PROFITS OF CRIME AND THEIR RECOVERY

CAMBRIDGE STUDIES IN CRIMINOLOGY

PROFITS OF CRIME AND THEIR RECOVERY

Report of a Committee chaired by
Sir Derek Hodgson

Heinemann · London

Published by Heinemann Educational Books Ltd
22 Bedford Square, London WC1 3HH

ISBN 0 435 82650 6

Typeset by Inforum Ltd, Portsmouth
and printed by Biddles Ltd, Guildford, Surrey

Contents

Members of the Committee

Sir Derek Hodgson, one of Her Majesty's judges of the Queen's Bench Division of the High Court – Chairman

Andrew Nicol, barrister and lecturer-in-law at the London School of Economics and Political Science – Secretary

Louis Blom-Cooper QC, Chairman of the Howard League for Penal Reform

Martin Iredale, chartered accountant, partner in W.H. Cork Gully & Co.

N. Anthony Leifer, solicitor, partner in D.J. Freeman & Co.

Deputy Assistant Commissioner J.M. Sewell QPM, Metropolitan Police

Clive Soley, Labour MP for Hammersmith

Sir Christopher Staughton, one of Her Majesty's judges of the Queen's Bench Division of the High Court

Professor Nigel Walker CBE, Cambridge Institute of Criminology

J. Selwyn Nottingham of the Home Office attended as an observer

Acknowledgements

The work of the Committee has been financed by the Howard League for Penal Reform and by two donations. The Nuffield Foundation gave us £2000 out of which it has been possible modestly to reimburse the secretariat and to pay for members' travelling expenses. The Hilden Charity provided £1000 towards the expenses of four members who attended a three-day seminar in Ottawa in January 1983 organised by the Solicitor-General's Department of the Government of Canada. Much that appears in chapter 4 results from discussions there with North American experts on the jurisdictions on that continent.

The Committee hopes that its report will be widely discussed. We have been fortunate in finding that our publishers, Heinemann Educational Books, regard it as worthy of inclusion in its Cambridge Studies in Criminology Series, under the general editorship of Sir Leon Radzinowicz, the first Director of the Institute of Criminology and Wolfson Professor of Criminology at the University of Cambridge. The publishers' editor, Mr David Hill, has been exceptionally helpful in translating the manuscript into a handsome publication.

The Committee has been very fortunate in its secretary, Mr Andrew Nicol, who is a practising barrister and a lecturer in the Law Department of the London School of Economics. Mr Nicol did all the research upon which our consultation document was based. By his later work both in research and in the organisation of very disparate material he has contributed inestimably to the Committee's deliberations. The preparation of minutes and collation of material are further tasks which he has performed with skill and efficiency. He has also written a number of draft chapters for the consideration of the Committee. The clarity of his writing has greatly facilitated the final stages of the Report. No committee can have been better served. Our thanks must also go to his research assistant, Miss Alison Real.

Mr Nicol's contribution to the work of the Committee has not been limited to his duties as secretary. The promoters invited him to serve also as a full member of the Committee and he has thus been able to make an even more significant contribution to the Committee's deliberations.

The London School of Economics has provided facilities for our meetings and we held two all-day meetings in accommodation provided by the Honourable Society of the Middle Temple.

viii   *Profits of Crime and their Recovery*

Last, and by no means least, our grateful thanks are due to Mrs Jane Heginbotham who provided the secretarial back-up. She has attended our committee meetings, taken shorthand notes, reproduced the minutes, and done all the typing of the many manuscripts. Our work would have been impossible without her unfailing efficiency.

Part One

1 Introduction

In the summer of 1978 a case which came to be known as the 'Operation Julie' case (after one of the policewomen involved in the investigation) was tried in the Crown Court at Bristol. Those convicted at the trial had over a number of years, and on a vast scale, manufactured and sold the hallucinogenic drug lysergic acid, more commonly known as LSD. The case attracted a great deal of public attention. The offenders were sentenced to long terms of imprisonment. In addition the Judge made an order, confirmed by the Court of Appeal, for the forfeiture of certain assets in their hands purportedly exercising a power given by sect. 27(1) of the Misuse of Drugs Act 1971. Huge profits had been made, and the prosecution was able to trace some £750,000 of those profits to assets in the criminals' hands. These assets included cash, cars, deposits of money and securities at bank accounts in Switzerland and France, rights and interests in a post office savings account, a debt due to one of the gang, paintings and electrical equipment. The power given to the Court under the Act was to 'order anything shown to the satisfaction of the Court to relate to the offence to be forfeited'.

A further appeal was made to the House of Lords against the orders for forfeiture and the House 'with considerable regret' found itself compelled to allow the appeals. Among the reasons given for allowing the appeal the House held that Parliament had never intended orders of forfeiture to 'serve as a means of stripping the drug traffickers of the total profits of their unlawful enterprises'. The power could only be used where it was 'possible to identify something tangible that can fairly be said to relate to any such transaction such as the drugs involved, apparatus for making them, vehicles used for transporting them or cash ready to be or having just been handed over for them'. The House also held that an English court has no jurisdiction to make orders for the transfer of property situated abroad; and that no order could be made under sect. 27 (1) because the defendants were charged not with offences under the Act but with conspiracy to commit them.[1]

The apparent inability of the Court effectively to deprive an offender of the profits of his offending caused substantial public concern, particularly when it was realised that there were many other criminal

1. *R v. Cuthbertson* [1981] A.C. 470 for the Court of Appeal's decision see *R. v. Kemp and Others* (1979) 69 Cr. App. R. 330.

activities where huge profits were made and the Court's powers were similarly restricted. Nor, it was realised, were the courts in any better position where the offences committed were of less glaring criminality. Large profits can result from the contravention of regulatory provisions, and the power of the Court to impose monetary penalties is often wholly insufficient substantially to touch them.

There is equal concern even more frequently articulated over what is seen as an obsession with the criminal and neglect of his victim. But the emphasis is often placed not so much on helping the victim as on satisfying what are thought to be his feelings and fears by increasing the retribution exacted upon the offender. A great deal more could, and we believe should, be done to help the victims of crime. The total amount of financial assistance provided by government for the many victim support schemes which have been set up in recent years amounted in 1982/3 to £29,000.[2]

The Howard League works for reform of the criminal justice system. Its concern extends both to the question of taking from offenders the profits of crime and assisting its victims. The League believed that examination of the law with a view to its reform in these two respects would involve complex issues which deserved review in the context of the whole armoury of the Court's powers to make monetary and proprietary orders. Therefore, under its auspices but entirely independent of it, our Committee was formed and given this remit:

To consider the present law relating to the forfeiture of property associated with crime, in the light of the House of Lords' judgment in *R v. Cuthbertson and Others*, 12 June 1980; to consider the law and procedure relating to compensation and restitution of property to the victims of crime, and the operation of criminal bankruptcy; to assess how far the powers of criminal courts to impose monetary penalties meet the need to strip offenders of their illgotten gains, and whether further provisions are necessary to ensure that the fruits of crime are returned either to the innocent owners of property or to the Crown.

We have been encouraged and assisted in our work by the Home Office and Mr Selwyn Nottingham of that Department of State has attended nearly all our meetings as an observer and made most helpful contributions to our discussion.

At an early stage we realised that there was no generally accepted terminology to describe the various situations which we should have to examine. To some extent we have had to invent our own vocabulary and we have consequently attributed discrete meaning to terms which in ordinary speech might be treated as synonymous. The four words

2. However it is fair to note that the state's main contribution to victims of crimes of violence is the sum of about £29 million paid to the Criminal Injuries Compensation Board. See further p. 49.

we use are 'forfeiture', 'compensation', 'restitution' and 'confiscation'.

By *forfeiture* we mean the power of the Court to take property that is immediately connected with an offence. Spread throughout our law there are very many specific powers of forfeiture such as the one unsuccessfully sought to be exercised in the Operation Julie case. There is also a general power contained in sect. 43 of the Powers of Criminal Courts Act 1973.

We use *compensation* to refer to financial reparation to a victim by an offender for loss, injury, suffering or damage resulting from an offence. Sects. 35 to 38 of the 1973 Act contain the principal powers of the criminal courts to award compensation.

Restitution is used to mean the return of property or its monetary equivalent to the person from whom it was unlawfully taken. The power to order restitution is found in Section 28 of the Theft Act 1968 and to magistrates by the Police (Property) Act 1897.

Finally, *confiscation* is taken to mean the depriving of an offender of the proceeds or the profits of crime. It was the inability of the courts to order confiscation in this sense which was highlighted by the Operation Julie case.

We began our work by publishing a consultative paper which was given a wide circulation. Following upon that paper and based upon it we have had many meetings with individuals and the representatives of organisations interested in its subject matter. We also received a large number of written comments. (For a list of written and oral submissions see p. 159.) We are very grateful for all these submissions, which whether or not they are specifically cited have been of great assistance.

Our consideration of forfeiture, in the narrow sense we have given the word, and of restitution may seem to be of a largely technical nature. The present state of the law can best be described as incoherent and from its tangled provisions anomalies have been thrown up and inconsistencies revealed. We have found, though, that issues of principle often lie under the surface of this 'lawyer's law'. Our recommendations will, we hope, help to identify the problem and indicate ways of making these two weapons in the armoury of the courts more effective.

The discussions we have had among ourselves and with others on the subject of confiscation and compensation have been much more wide-ranging, innovatory and of a broadly jurisprudential nature, particularly in relation to confiscation. We cannot pretend that we have been able to devise any easy answers. Attacking the profits of organised 'non-victim' crime and contraventions of regulations presents profound difficulties which we have not been able fully to resolve but we hope that the consideration we have given to the subject and the tentative proposals we make will stimulate discussion and lead eventually to effective means being provided to enable the courts to ensure that crime does not pay.

While we do not in this introduction to our Report wish to foreshadow the detailed consideration which we give to the various aspects of our remit we do think that it may be helpful and of interest if at this early stage we state in general terms some of the principles that underlie our thinking. They were either with us when we began our task or have emerged and achieved consensus during our discussions.

Imprisonment as a response to serious crime is no longer the automatic reaction of our criminal justice system. It is not only the present overloading of the prison system which has led to this change. We have less confidence in the deprivation of liberty as a general deterrent, especially when the probability of its imposition is so low because of the difficulties of detection. Nor is there any longer much confidence in imprisonment as a means of reform. Even as an individual deterrent its effectiveness seems to be limited and such individual deterrence as it may possess becomes rapidly less and less effective with repetition. Mere containment has largely taken over from treatment as the function of prison and the belief that you can in some way 'improve' a human being after you have taken away his liberty has been heavily eroded in recent times. It is against this background of what may be called 'penological pessimism' that we have approached our task.

We believe that too much attention is paid to punishment and too little to redressing the wrong done and that nothing like enough consideration is given to the victim in the criminal process. We find much wisdom in the writings of Jeremy Bentham. 'Compensation', he wrote 'will answer the purpose of punishment but punishment will not answer the purpose of compensation. By compensation therefore the two great ends of justice are both answered at a time, by punishment only once.'[3] In his 'Principles of Legislation' he further declared that punishment that went beyond the limit of necessity was a pure evil. He said that in his time – and we believe it to be no less true today – punishment 'had been scattered with a prodigal hand' whereas satisfaction which he declared as purely a good had been dealt out 'with the most evident parsimony'.[4] Any resort to imprisonment can be justified only to the extent that the exaction of pecuniary penalties

3. Ms portfolio 98 f.4.
4. p. 284.

in the form either of victim redress or the confiscation of the fruits of crime is inadequate. As Bentham himself put it 'the value of the punishment must not be less in any case than what is efficient to outweigh that of the profits of the offence'.[5] The aim must be to construct a system of redress that is adequate to obviate as far as possible the necessity of resort to the sanction of imprisonment.

There is nothing new in the concept of redress by an offender, either for the loss or damage he has caused to his victim or for the profit he has made. What is comparatively new is the intensified search for appropriate methods of achieving the laudable social objective of redress for crime.

Redress for the victims of crime has been unhelpfully affected by the division of the law into crimes and civil wrongs. Jursiprudential commentators have through the ages debated the significance and the wisdom of that division. Lord Mansfield in *Atcheson v. Evitt*[6] declared that there was 'no distinction better known, than the distinction between civil and criminal law'. Later, by contrast, the Utilitarian philosophers, Bentham and Austin, commented that both civil and penal sanctions were mostly 'related evils'. For Bentham it was 'most manifest' that 'no settled line can be drawn between the civil branch and the penal'[7] and Austin contended that 'the differences between civil injuries and crimes can hardly be found in any difference between the ends or purposes of the corresponding sanctions.'[8] The essential homogeneity of the two distinct branches of the law was expounded by Mr Justice Holmes in his classical work, *The Common Law*; he simply asserted that 'the general principles of criminal and civil liability are the same',[9] thus rejecting the traditional distinction propounded by Blackstone which marked out punishment from redress.[10] Criminologists of the positivist school at the turn of the century similarly pointed out that the separation of criminal and civil law was illogical, there being no essential difference between the two branches.[11] The debate among criminologists, however, has persisted;[12]

Administrators in post-war Britain, on the other hand, have ack-

---

5. *On Morals and Legislation*, Vol. II, Chapter XIV, p. 16.
6. (1775) 1 Cowp. 382, 391: 98 E.R. 1142, 1147.
7. *Limits of Jurisprudence Defined*, (C. Everett, ed., 1945) 298.
8. *Lectures on Jurisprudence*, (R. Campbell, 4th edn., 1973). 520.
9. (1881) p. 44.
10. Blackstone's 'Commentaries' IV 5.7.
11. Ferri, *Criminal Sociology* (J. Kelly trans., 1917), pp. 411–13; and Garofalo, *Criminology* (R. Miller trans., 1914), pp. 419–35.
12. See Harland, 'Monetary Remedies for the Victims of Crime: Assessing the role of the Criminal Courts', (1982) 30 UCLA Law Review 401–77, esp. pp. 402 n. 9.

nowledged that the forum of the criminal court is an entirely appropriate place for victim redress. A significant government White Paper of 1959[13] declared that the concept of personal reparation by an offender would have to be considered in the context of a fundamental re-examination of penal philosophy and practice.[14]

Further impetus towards securing better means of depriving offenders of the fruits of crime came in 1966 in the evidence of the Law Society to the Royal Commission on the Penal System. This commission was set up in 1964 by the outgoing Conservative administration and unprecedentedly dissolved in 1966 (by the incoming Labour administration) to be replaced by the Home Secretary's Advisory Council on the Penal System (itself lapsing in 1980). In their evidence the Law Society floated the novel idea of criminal bankruptcy. In one of its early reports[15] the Advisory Council, in taking on board the idea of criminal bankruptcy, proclaimed the new philosophy which has permeated thought and action in recent times, in the ritual abandonment in practice, but not in theory, of the civil process as a means of providing redress for crime. It concluded that 'if any advance is to be made it is to the criminal court that we must look'.[16]

Four years later the view expressed by the Council was echoed by the Law Reform Commission of Canada, which suggested that restitution should assume a central role in criminal sentencing.[17] A clear judicial preference in America for restitution within the criminal justice system is also reflected in the Model Penal Code.[18]

It is the conventional wisdom of sound parental teaching that crime does not pay. Stripped of the twin elements of nursery room rhetoric and parental admonition to the child that even financial gain from unacceptable social behaviour will bring about neither spiritual rewards nor a proper development of individual character in adulthood, the essential lesson about law-abiding behaviour remains. Society and its laws require that the 'criminal should pay'. To accommodate this homespun philosophy every reasonable effort needs to be made to require the offender to make amends and to recognise that victims should not suffer financial loss. The retort, that the victim can

13. *Penal Practice in a Changing Society; Aspects of Future Development (England and Wales)* Cmnd 645.
14. *Ibid.*, paras 25–7.
15. *Reparation by the Offender*, (1970).
16. *Ibid.*, p. 56.
17. *Restitution and Compensation*, pp. 5–8.
18. Proposed Official Draft 1962 para 301.1(2) (1): see also Model Sentencing Act (para 9, National Council on Crime and Delinquency, 2nd edn. 1972) and a recent draft of the proposed new Federal Criminal Codes (Criminal Code Revision Act of 1979, sect. 1723, 96th Congress, 1st Session, para 3102(a)93). (Restitution declared to be one of the 'purposes of sentencing'.)

always bring a civil action against the defendant for the recovery of the loss resulting from a criminal act, ignores the financial inability and the lack of litigious stamina of the majority of victims to sustain a civil suit. At present criminal justice is administered principally for the protection of the whole of society. Its concern for the individual victim should not be merely incidental to that purpose; such concern is central to society's need in order that the collective purpose may be served.

Excluding crimes of violence where containment in prison may be the only way in which society can be protected, there are three broad categories of illegal conduct from which substantial gains can be made. These are 'victim' crimes, the paradigms of which are fraud and theft; there are 'non-victim' crimes, for example the drug and pornography rackets, unlawful gaming, the transportation of illegal immigrants and the corruption of officials; and there are those regulatory offences that involve less obvious criminality; for example the property developer who enormously increases the value of his land by demolishing a listed building or cutting down protected trees, the haulier who overloads his lorries, the manufacturer who pollutes a river with his industrial effluent, or the trader who systematically contravenes the rules of fair trading. The profits made out of this last method of transgressing the law can be enormous and the fines imposed are frequently derisory in comparison; the fine which can be imposed is often a very cheap price to pay for the profit made.

An attempt was made to deal with serious victim-crime by the introduction (as a result of a recommendation by the Advisory Council on the Penal System) of the Criminal Bankruptcy Order. Unfortunately, this addition to the armoury of the criminal courts has proved almost wholly ineffective and is infrequently used. It is conceptually wrong because the whole basis upon which it is made is that the offender is not bankrupt but wrongfully solvent and the necessity of precisely identifying the amount owed and to whom has presented the authorities with frequently insurmountable problems.

With one exception no serious attempt is made to redress the harm done and profit made by the second and third category of offending. The exception is the procedures adopted by the Inland Revenue and Customs and Excise which provide in effect for the confiscation of the gains of offenders guilty of offences of immediately recognisable criminality. While the effectiveness of these procedures may point a way forward to the more general use of comparable procedures in the criminal law their present unique position is socially significant because it reflects a disturbing discrimination between classes of offenders. By the payment of penalties the fraudulent evader of taxes escapes the obloquy of a criminal conviction, a privilege denied to the shoplifter or the embezzler. If society is content that a tax fraudster should escape conviction by the payment of a penalty, why not also the porn merchant, the corrupter of officials and the transporter of illegal immigrants, not to mention the type of petty offender referred to above?

If redress is seen as having greater importance in our criminal process and the victims of crime as having an essential role to play there are implications throughout the whole of that process, investigation, prosecution and disposal. We seek in this context to look at all those stages.

Another aspect of victim-support which we have had at the front of our mind during our work is the danger that increasing the powers of the Court to redress the results of serious or profitable crime may have unintended consequences in relation to low income offenders. The ability of an offender to pay a monetary penalty, whether by way of fine, compensation or confiscation is something which we believe is of great importance if the infliction of the penalty is not to have the effect of driving the offender into further offending or of imposing undue hardship on his or her innocent family. It is not enough to assume that the Court, particularly the magistrates' court, adequately takes this into account. The loss of a job, or professional disciplining, or the inability to pay other debts such as rent or electricity accounts are often not brought to the attention of the court. Usually this is no doubt due to a failure by the defendant to give this information either to the police or to the probation service.

Our resources have seriously limited our work in the field of comparative law. We have nevertheless amassed a great deal of material as to what the law is and some information as to the trends being taken in other countries. We did not, however, have the resources to conduct much useful research into how the law operates in practice in those countries, and so have been able to do no more than in some cases refer to secondary sources.

The field of our enquiry has been wide and the canvas we seek to paint is a broad one. Necessarily many of the topics we have considered overlap and important questions have application to more than one of the separate aspects we have looked at. Our aim has been to impede as little as possible the general flow of argument without too much repetition or references back or forward. But because of the interaction between so many of the separate subjects we have examined, complete success in attaining this objective has not been possible.

We begin by looking briefly at the historical background in English law to the objects of our study. We have devoted a chapter to the powers of the civil courts which are analogous to the powers of the criminal courts either already in existence or which we recommend. Before turning to consider in detail the different subjects of our enquiry, we take a necessarily cursory look at the relevant law in other countries.

Next we deal with the two aspects of our remit which are most near the heart of our main concerns, that victims should be compensated and that crime should not pay, compensation and confiscation. This is followed by an investigation of the courts' powers to order restitution and to forfeit property immediately connected with an offence. Out of these matters there arise common questions both of principle and practice which merit separate consideration. Consequently we next turn to questions which are more of a procedural nature, pre-trial restraint, criminal bankruptcy, the assessment of means, the interests of third parties and the application of moneys or properties received. We then look at an important question of principle, namely the relationship between monetary and proprietary orders and penalties which are purely punitive. Finally we consider briefly the international aspects of our enquiry.

2 Historical background

(1) Feudal forfeiture

Medieval criminal courts did not make orders of compensation or confiscation in serious cases. This was not because of indifference to the victim or tenderness to the offender but because *all* of the property of a convicted felon was forfeited. In feudal theory, rights over land, the most important form of property, were intimately connected with correlative duties of loyalty, obedience and allegiance to the superior lord of whom the land was held, and to the king who alone 'owned' property rather than some tenure or estate in it. One explanation of the word 'felony' is that it was derived from the Saxon words 'fee' or landholding and 'lon' or price so that it meant in effect the crime which cost a person his property.[1] The felon's family were also deprived of any future interest or of any right of inheritance that came to them through him, for a further consequence of conviction was 'corruption of the blood'.

Forfeiture followed judgment[2] (usually of death) after conviction or, if the suspect fled, a judgment of outlawry. However, a conviction required a trial and a trial required a plea. A person who refused to plead was not released but subjected to the gruesome process of *peine forte et dure*, the gradual piling of rocks onto a board which was placed over his body and which continued until he gave his plea or died. The only attraction of the latter course was that the defendant died unconvicted and his family could succeed to the defendant's property.[3]

Whatever its theoretical underpinning, forfeiture became an important source of revenue for the Crown. It was the Crown which received all forfeited personal property.[4] It was also entitled to the land of convicted traitors. But for felonies other than treason it only had the right to waste the land for a year and a day before the property escheated to the felon's immediately superior feudal lord.[5] Valuable rights thus depended on whether a wrongdoer was prosecuted for

1. *Kenny's Outlines of the Criminal Law*, new 16th edn. by J.C.W. Turner (1952), para 73; Milsom, *Historical Foundations of the Common Law*, 2nd edn. (1981), p. 406.
2. Until judgment, the conviction might be set aside because, for instance, of a defect in the indictment. Blackstone's 'Commentaries' IV 380, 388.
3. In 1772 Parliament provided that silence should be taken as a plea of guilty. In 1827 this was amended to a plea of not guilty. 7 & 8 Geo 4.c. 28 sect. 2.
4. A. Steel, *The Receipt of the Exchequer 1377–1485* (1854).
5. Viner's *Abridgment*, 2nd edn. Vol. XII, pp. 436–57.

treason or felony and one of the Barons' grievances with King John was that he had extended the circumstances in which treason charges could be brought. In Magna Carta he undertook to do this no more[6] but later Edward III followed the same practice causing Parliament to take the rare step for those days of defining a crime by statute. The Treason Act of 1351 is still the basis of the offence today.

Medieval law saw victims of crime as having an important role in bringing offenders to justice. The owner of stolen goods lost all right to them unless he had been responsible for apprehending the thief. If he was not they went with other forfeited chattels to the Crown.[7] A statute of Henry VIII[8] changed this, but left unaffected a further incentive to prosecution. Stolen goods could normally be recovered from third parties unless they had been bought in good faith in a 'market overt'. However the original owner could reclaim his property even in this situation if, but only if, he had prosecuted the thief to conviction.[9] This remained the law until the Theft Act 1968 finally severed the link between participation in a prosecution and recovery of property.[10]

Those who suffered criminal violence or damage were caught in a double bind when it came to civil remedies. They were barred from bringing an action for a tort which also constituted a felony until after conviction.[11] Then, of course, it was too late since on conviction all the offender's property was forfeited. The courts grew more and more unhappy with this rule and connived at avoiding it.[12] To an extent it also inhibited the creation of new felonies unless, as in the case of the Riot Acts (which allowed mortal force to be used to dispel a felonious crowd) Parliament correspondingly expanded alternative means of compensation.[13] The rule did not apply to actions under the Fatal Accidents Act 1846[14], but it was not until the Criminal Law Act 1967 abolished the felony/misdemeanour categorisation that the formal bar to bringing an action was completely removed.[15]

---

6. Pollock and Maitland, *History of English Law* (1923 edn.) Vol. II., p. 500.
7. *Ibid.*, p. 165, unless the offender had been tried by battle (when this was still possible). Milson, *op. cit.*, p. 407.
8. 21 Hen. VIII c. 11. (1529).
9. The rule was codified by Parliament in the Sale of Goods Act 1893 sect. 24.
10. Theft Act 1968 s.33 (3) & Sched. 3.
11. Holdsworth, *History of English Law*, Vol. 10, p. 331–3; *Smith v. Selwyn* [1914] 3 K.B. 98.
12. See *Tyler v. Cork County Council* [1921] 2 I.R. 8, 19 per Sir James Campbell.
13. *Ibid.*, p. 17.
14. sect. 1.
15. The Criminal Law Revision Committee had recommended that no action be taken to preserve it when felonies were abolished and Parliament accordingly allowed it to die.

(2)   Deodand[16]

Distinct from forfeiture was the power of the court to seize as deodand
any object which caused a person's death. Of course, if the object was
the property of the killer and the homicide was felonious, it would
anyway be forfeited. Deodand was therefore only relevant where
death had been by misadventure, where the culprit could not be
identified or where a murder weapon belonged to a third party.
Deodand was recognised in Saxon times and before that in the Book of
Exodus we read, 'If an oxe gore a man or a woman that they die, then
the ox shall be surely stoned, and his flesh shall not be eaten; but the
owner of the ox shall be quit.'[17]

Even a tree from which a man accidentally fell to his death was
susceptible to being felled and confiscated. An old couplet ran

Whatever moved to do the deed
Is deodand and forfeited.

The principle behind deodand was a primitive attempt to punish
the guilty object, as a means of channelling a desire for revenge, and of
symbolising the community's loss from a premature death.[18] It was
not initially a means of compensating the victim's family, for the
object or rather its value was forfeited to the Crown. It has been
suggested that 'deodand' derives from Deo Dandum – to be given to
God[19] – and by the Middles Ages, at least, deodands were sold and
applied to 'pious uses'. The Royal Almoner was given notional res-
ponsibility for collecting the Crown's due but, for cash or favour, the
right to receive local deodands was often granted to others. After the
Reformation, at least some of the proceeds would be customarily
given to the relatives.

Coroners' juries determined exactly what property was deodand (a
nice point in the case, for instance, of a large machine with some parts
moving and some static) and its value. They were left considerable
latitude in fixing the latter. By the early nineteenth century it was
rarely fixed at more than a few shillings, though the object could have
been sold on the market for much more. Occasionally, a particularly
outrageous fatality would move the jury into fixing a higher amount.
A hit-and-run coach which killed a passerby in Pimlico was assessed at

16. Kenny, *op. cit.*, para 7. Holdsworth, *History of English Law*, Vol. 10, p. 351;
    Holmes, *The Common Law*, chapter 1; Pollock and Maitland, *History of English
    Law* (2nd edn. 1909), p. 473.
17. chapter 21, verse 28.
18. Finkelstein, 'The Gored Ox: Some Historial Perspectives on Deodands, For-
    feitures, Wrongful Death and the Western Notion of Sovereignty' (1973) 46
    Temple Law Quarterly 169.
19. *Calero-Toledo v. Pearson Yacht & Leasing Co.* 416 U.S. 663, 681 (1974) (US
    Sup. Ct).

£20. Ironically, this penalty would not have been borne by the driver (who remained unidentified) but by the local community which was responsible for paying uncollected deodands.[20]

Deodand provided crude and arbitrary compensation for bereaved families, but it had its advantages. It was quick and cheap and applied, potentially, to any death. It was not, for instance, until the Motor Insurers' Bureau was set up that families of a person killed by an unknown 'hit-and-run' driver could obtain any other compensation.

(3) Abolition of forfeiture and deodand

By the nineteenth century, forfeiture and deodand had become anachronistic royal prerogatives. The original theory of the feudal bond was outdated and the distinction between felonies and misdemeanours was no longer that between serious crimes and petty offences. It was thought unfair that a minor theft should entail forfeiture when a statutory fraud did not.

Forfeiture penalised the families of the convicted person, however little they may have had to do with the offence.[21] The property might be returned *ex gratia*, but only in a haphazard way. Thus of £1200 forfeited in 1864, £400 was returned, while of £1589 forfeited in 1868, £1112 was returned.[22] The victims of crime, as we have seen, were effectively deprived of any civil remedy since there were no assets out of which to pay damages. Creditors were less than happy that repayment of their debts depended on the Crown's indulgence. Some sympathy was also felt for timorous but innocent souls who transferred their estates to trustees to evade forfeiture and who, after their acquittal, had difficulty in recovering their property.[23] Finally forfeiture was no longer the profitable perquisite that it had once been. After 1814 corruption of the blood was abolished except for murder or treason so that (except in these cases) the convicted person's heirs could succeed to his property after his death.[24] Between 1848 and 1869 forfeiture never yielded more than £2070 to the Crown, and in its last year, 1869, gross receipts, before returns, were down to £530.[25] Most felons it seems were poor and the rich had found ways of salting their assets away before arrest.

Deodand, however, was the first of the two to go. In 1840,

20. Harry Smith, 'From Deodand to Dependency' (1967) 11 American Journal of American History, 389.
21. Hansard, 3rd series, Vol. 200, col. 931 *et seq.*
22. House of Commons Paper 125 (1870).
23. Hansard, Vol. 200, col. 933.
24. 54 Geo III c. 145 (1814).
25. H.C. 136 (1864) and H.C. 125 (1870).

deodands of between £500 and £2000 had been assessed on railway engines and carriages which had been involved in fatal accidents.[26] Lord Campbell proposed allowing dependants a general right to sue for wrongful death and, as a palliative, suggested that deodand should be ended. Parliament accepted the package and in 1846 the first Fatal Accident Act was passed and deodand was abolished.

The Statute Law Commissioners who were charged with planning a modern and revised set of statutes twice recommended that forfeiture should also be ended.[27] A government Bill passed the Commons without a division in 1866 but fell with a change in government. It was left to a private member, Charles Foster M.P., to introduce a bill in 1870 which, with government support, became the Felony Act 1870.[28] It has since been renamed the Forfeiture Act 1870. The Act abolished forfeiture, escheat, attainder, and corruption of the blood as a consequence of felony or treason. Convicts still lost rights to their property while undergoing penal servitude. An administrator was appointed with powers to deal with the property. He was in a fiduciary position, had to act bona fide and return what was left at the end of the sentence. These provisions were repealed in 1948.[29]

Curiously, due to government pressure the 1870 bill specifically preserved forfeiture consequent upon outlawry which had last been imposed in 1859.[30] This survived in theory until 1938.[31] A few misdemeanours for which forfeiture was prescribed by statute also slipped the 1870 net until repealed by the Criminal Law Act 1967.[32]

There were those who grumbled at the passing of forfeiture. Holdsworth wrote:

The modern state has found that confiscation by means of death duties of a considerable part of the property of its most prosperous and generally its most deserving citizens, is a far more lucrative source of revenue than the confiscation of the whole of the property of the generally impecunious persons who have been found guilty of the more heinous variety of crimes. Envy of the deserving because they are rich and sympathy with the poor because they are criminals are characteristics of the perverted vision of democracy.[33]

26. Harry Smith, *op. cit.*
27. According to Charles Forster, the M.P. who introduced the 1870 Felony Bill: Hansard, 3rd Series, Vol. 200, col. 931.
28. 33 & 34 Vict. c. 23.
29. Criminal Justice Act 1948 sect. 70(1).
30. H. Erle Richards, 'Is Outlawry Obsolete' (1902) 18 LQR 297.
31. Administration of Justice (Miscellaneous Provisions) Act, 1938 sect. 12.
32. See the 7th Report of the Criminal Law Revision Committee on Felonies and Misdemeanours, Cmnd 2659.
33. *History of English Law*, Vol. 10, p. 351.

(4) Statutory forfeiture

Even while feudal forfeiture survived, the courts were given statutory powers to forfeit specific kinds of property because of its immediate connection with certain offences. Broadly speaking these fell into two classes. The first was where possession of the object was itself an offence, e.g. the tools for making counterfeit currency and the coins themselves. With the proliferation of bans or restrictions on certain kinds of commercial dealings this first category grew rapidly. Legislation concerning poaching, street betting, pornography, fish conservation and prohibited drugs all included forfeiture provisions (and do so now). As more attention was focused on preventative offences, these powers were correspondingly broadened. Offensive weapons became forfeitable, as did the equipment for making prohibited drugs.[34]

The second type of specific forfeiture power was a means of enforcing fiscal policies. For centuries the customs authorities have had power to seize and forfeit contraband and conveyances used in smuggling. A similar tradition lies behind their equivalent present powers to forfeit alcoholic drinks, tobacco and oil products on which duty has not been paid or property connected with the evasion.[35]

These specific statutory powers can be divided along another plane. In some cases they were (and are) only exercisable after the owner has been found guilty of the relevant offence. Offensive weapons, for instance, can only be forfeited after a conviction, whereas tools for making forgeries or false instruments may be taken whether or not criminal proceedings are instituted.[36]

In 1970 the Advisory Council on the Penal System recommended that these post-conviction forfeiture powers should be generalised.[37] This recommendation was adopted and is now contained in sect. 43 of Powers of Criminal Courts Act 1973. Consequently whenever a person is convicted of an offence carrying more than two years' imprisonment the Court may forfeit any interest which he has in property that was used or intended to be used for committing or facilitating the commission of any offence. This power was in addition to, not in replacement

34. See now, for instance, Deer Act 1980 sect. 5, Deer Act 1963 sect. 6(3), Game Laws (Amendment) Act 1960 sect. 4, Betting Gaming and Lotteries Act 1963 sect. 8; Obscene Publications Act 1959 sect. 3; Salmon and Freshwater Fisheries Act 1975 Sched 4 para 5; Misuse of Drugs Act 1971 sect. 27; Prevention of Crime Act 1951 sect. 1(2).
35. Customs and Excise Management Act 1979 – various sections; Alcoholic Liquor Duties Act 1979; Hydrocarbon Oil Duties Act 1979; Matches and Mechanical Lighters Duties Act 1979; Tobacco Product Duties Act 1979.
36. Prevention of Crime Act 1951 sect. 1(2); Forgery and Counterfeiting Act 1981 sect. 7.
37. Report of Sub-Committee chaired by Lady Barbara Wootton 'Non-Custodial and Semi-Custodial Sentences' (1970), paras 145–9.

of the earlier legislation. Further specific forfeiture powers have been enacted since 1973. Such powers are now included in over fifty different statutes. A question considered later is whether it is time to rationalise them into a single comprehensive provision.

Customs and revenue forfeitures have never been dependent on criminal convictions. They have always taken the form of civil or rather quasi-criminal proceedings. Originally they were brought in the Court of Exchequer.[38] In chapter 8 we refer in more detail to the present position. Certain other things such as counterfeit coins or forged banknotes – the very existence of which constituted a threat to the public interest – are also forfeitable by magistrates acting in a quasi-criminal capacity.[39] It was by analogy with such inherently dangerous things that obscene publications were first subjected to forfeiture in 1857.[40] We examine these specific powers of forfeiture in their present-day form in chapter 8.

(5) Compensation

In marked distinction from the practice in civil law countries, compensation was the concern of the civil courts rather than those of criminal jurisdiction.[41] Moreover, as we have seen, if the offence was a felony, the defendant would be stripped of all his property and have nothing out of which to pay compensation. The separation of criminal and civil functions was maintained even in the case of lesser offences or misdemeanours. The victim might institute criminal proceedings, but thereafter they were conducted in the name of the Crown. This attitude of the King's common law courts was in sharp contrast to the local courts which did combine compensation with punishment. The Star Chamber likewise dealt with both aspects in one proceeding but with the absorption of both into the common law system, this omnibus approach to wrongs was lost.[42]

The expense of civil actions, even in the cheaper county courts which were established in 1846, and the paucity of means of most offenders stimulated Parliament to confer a limited jurisdiction on the criminal courts to make an order of compensation. At first these, like the provisions regarding restitution of stolen property, were rewards

38. James R. Maxeiner, 'Bane of American Forfeiture Law – Banished at Last' (1977) 62 Cornell Law Review 768.
39. Forgery and Counterfieting Act 1981 sects. 7 and 24.
40. Obscene Publications Act 1857; see Geoffrey Robertson, *Obscenity* (1979), pp. 26–33.
41. A difference regretted by Lord Wilberforce in *DPP v. Anderson* [1978] 2 All ER 512, 514.
42. Milsom, *Historical Foundations of the Common Law* (1981), pp. 320, 405, 418–19.

for those who had assisted in bringing offenders to justice.[43] A statute of 1826 gave (and gives) the court power to pay compensation for 'expenses, exertion, loss of time in or towards such apprehension' to a witness or to the family of a person killed while attempting to capture a suspect.[44] In 1861, the Malicious Damage Act allowed the owner of damaged property to obtain some recompense.[45] After feudal forfeiture was abolished in 1870, the convicted person could be ordered to pay compensation of up to £100 for loss of property.[46] The Summary Jurisdiction Act 1879 gave magistrates a very restricted power to order the payment of damages to the victim of a minor assault.

The increasing concern with the victims of crime has led to a recent expansion of these powers. In 1967 the Criminal Law Revision Committee recommended that the 1870 power be carried over to any indictable offence (magistrates had by then a comparable jurisdiction). They also recommended that it should be extended to property damage as well as loss and that the maximum should be raised from £100 to £400. Loss or damage arising out of the presence of a vehicle on the road ought to be excluded. They feared that the criminal courts would be bogged down in deciding issues of quantum and contributory negligence. These proposals were adopted in the Criminal Law Act 1967.[47]

The Advisory Council on the Penal System[48] endorsed the principle of criminal courts making compensation orders in simple cases and recommended that they be extended yet further, principally to include personal injury, and any other loss arising out of the commission of an offence. Parliament followed its recommendation in the Criminal Justice Act 1972 and the powers are now codified in Powers of Criminal Courts Act sects. 35–8 and the Criminal Justice Act 1982.

43. The offender could also be ordered to pay a reward to the person responsible for his apprehension under a wide variety of specific statutes until the Common Informers Act 1951 commuted all these into a power to impose a fine. In the United States similar powers still exist especially in relation to situations where property is forfeited from the offender. 19 U.S.C. 1619, for instance, provides in relation to drug-related forfeitures: 'Any person not an officer of the U.S. who detects and seizes any [property] subject to seizure and forfeiture . . . or who furnishes . . . original information . . . which leads to a . . . forfeiture . . . may be awarded 25% of the net amount recovered . . . not to exceed $50,000 . . . in any case.'
44. Criminal Law Act 1826 sects. 28–30. The moneys are paid out of public funds.
45. Sect. 52.
46. Forfeiture Act 1870 section 4.
47. Sched. 2 para 9.
48. Report of sub-committee chaired by Lord Widgery C.J. *Reparation by the Offender* (1970).

3   Civil analogues

The focus of our work has been the range of powers available to the criminal courts to compensate victims of crime, to confiscate illicit proceeds, to forfeit property immediately connected with offences and to restore property to its rightful owners. However, the significance of these powers, and their deficiencies, can only be understood in the context of the law as a whole. This chapter will, therefore, comment briefly on the analogous powers of civil courts. It is also worth studying the experience of civil courts in, for instance, depriving wrongdoers of improper gains or in temporarily freezing a defendant's assets prior to trial, before considering recommendations to give criminal courts comparable jurisdiction. Finally, we highlight the penal character of some aspects of our civil law.

(1)   Compensation

Most crimes are also torts or civil wrongs and give their victims a right to sue for damages. Thus crimes of violence are also the torts of assault and battery; theft and malicious damage will normally involve wrongful trespass to goods; and fraud entails both criminal and civil liability.

Generally speaking victims of crime face the same difficulties in using the civil system as other plaintiffs. It is an expensive process. In addition to their own legal bills they must assess the risk of losing and then being faced with the defendant's legal costs. In the case of small claims (under £500) this risk can be reduced by bringing them before the County Court registrars and asking them to act as arbitrators.[1] This is a less formal and intimidating procedure, and the loser does not normally have to pay for the cost of the winner's legal representation.[2] Equally, of course, it means that the plaintiffs must either manage their claims on their own, pay for lawyers out of their own pockets without hope of reimbursement or depend on the meagre assistance which solicitors can give under the 'Green Form' legal aid and advice scheme. This allows up to £50 of advice either free or subject to a means-tested contribution.[3]

1. County Court Rules 1981 Order 19 r.2(3). Up to £500 either party can insist on the matter being arbitrated (subject to a residual discretion in limited cases). By agreement between the parties, larger claims can be dealt with in this way as well but the costs limitation does not then apply (see note 2).
2. *Ibid.*, Order 19 r. 6.
3. Legal Aid Act 1974 sects. 1–4.

In cases of large or complex claims litigants can obtain legal aid subject to a means-tested contribution. Legal aid then covers the full cost of legal representation. Area Legal Aid Committees determine applications on the basis of whether a privately-paying litigant would think it worth pursuing.[4] Many applications are rejected because the likely level of damages is out of proportion to the probable cost. Even if the Committee is prepared to grant legal aid, the victim may still gain little by proceeding. This is because the costs that successful litigants are reimbursed by their opponents represent only a proportion (there is wide variation but 2/3 is about average) of the actual costs. The Legal Aid Committee has a statutory right to claim the difference out of any award of damages.[5] In consequence if the action is likely to be defended and the likely judgment less than about £1000, there will be little left for the victim after the Legal Aid Committee's claim has been met.

A victim of crime shares with other civil plaintiffs the further difficulty that effectively his claim is only as good as his defendant's pocket is deep. The development of an employer's vicarious liability for the damage caused by his employee's wrongs committed in the course of his employment has to a limited degree eased this difficulty. Compulsory liability insurance for drivers and employers has had a similar effect. Although victims are not parties to these contracts of insurance they have, by legislation, a direct right of action against an insurer if the insured is unable to pay the appropriate compensation.[6] As a result of government pressure, motor insurance companies have formed the Motor Insurers' Bureau to meet claims for personal injury arising out of negligent driving by uninsured or unidentified drivers.[7]

Victims of crime do have one advantage if the offender has been convicted. Since 1968, the conviction has been admissible as evidence in subsequent civil proceedings.[8] It is not conclusive evidence,[9] but is

4. *Ibid.*, sects. 6–10.
5. *Ibid.*, sect. 9(6) and (9).
6. Third Parties (Rights Against Insurers) Act 1930 sect. 1; Road Traffic Act 1972 sects. 149–150; Policyholders' Protection Act 1975 sect. 7.
7. Motor Insurers' Bureau (Compensation of Victims of Untraced Drivers) (1972); Motor Insurers' Bureau (Compensation of Victims of Uninsured Drivers) (1972); see *Hardy* v. *M.I.B.* [1964] 2 QB. 745; *White v. London Transport* [1971] 2 QB 721; *Persson v. London Country Buses* [1974] 1 All ER 1251.
8. Civil Evidence Act 1968 sect. 11, reversing the decision of the Court of Appeal in *Hollington v. Hewthorn* [1943] KB 581 and following the proposal of the Law Reform Committee in its 15th Report, Cmnd 3391.
9. The Law Reform Committee rejected the idea that a conviction should be conclusive evidence (1) because the evidence before the criminal court may have been incomplete (either because of the absence of proper representation or the defence may not otherwise have been most effectively presented) (2) the court may have made unreasonable inferences of fact and (3) the inconvenience, embarrassment and the size of penalty might have induced the defendant not to contest the charge or not to appeal the conviction. *Ibid.*, para 30.

likely to carry great weight. There is also the great advantage that it will have been obtained at the state's expense. On the other hand, parallel civil proceedings are likely to be delayed until the criminal prosecution is concluded.[10]

Compensation is provided not only by the civil courts. Social security may partially alleviate the loss in the form of unemployment, sickness benefit and, depending on the victim's means, supplementary benefit. The Criminal Injuries Compensation Board may also provide compensation (see further chapter 5).

(2)   Restitution and confiscation

Civil actions can be used to recover stolen or fraudulently obtained property, but they are not usually necessary when the property is found by the police in the course of their investigation. It will then be held as potential evidence and normally returned by the criminal court under the Theft Act 1968 sect. 28 or the Police (Property) Act 1897 (see further chapter 7).

But not every profitable crime has an identifiable victim. Traders in illegal drugs or obscene publications, for instance, cannot be sued by their customers. Even if the customer is dissatisfied with the product or cheated by the dealer, he will have no claim, for the law will not generally enforce an illegal contract nor assist in unscrambling one. There are exceptions to this rule,[11] but they are relatively unimportant. *A fortiori*, if the customer does receive what he bargained for, he has no right to recover his money: his purchase may be illegal, but his payment is effective and irrevocable.

10. It is a matter of discretion as to whether concurrent civil proceedings about the same subject-matter as a prosecution are stayed. The Court must decide whether justice between the parties requires this. It will have regard *inter alia* to the possibility of prejudicial publicity from the civil proceedings, whether the criminal trial is imminent and whether there is a real danger that the defendant would be prejudiced by being forced to disclose his defence to the criminal charge prematurely. *Jefferson Ltd v. Bhetcha* [1979] 1 WLR 898. cf. Supreme Court Practice, Vol. 2, para 3355 (1982 edn.).

11. See Treital, *The Law of Contract*, 6th edn., pp. 371–9. In brief money, or property can be recovered by the customer if
   (a) the customer repents after payment but before receipt of the prohibited goods. The change of heart must be true contrition and not pragmatic regret. *Alexander v. Rayson* [1936] 1 K.B. 169.
   (b) the transaction is prohibited under a statute intended to protect a weaker bargaining party or for some other reason the two are not *in pari delicto* e.g. *Kiriri Cotton Co. v. Dewani* [1960] A.C. 192, where the tenant was able to recover an illegal premium for a flat.
   (c) if only a limited interest was transferred and the customer can prove title to the goods independently of the contract e.g. *Bowmakers v. Barnet Instruments Ltd* [1945] K.B. 65.
   (d) If the recipient was guilty of fraud or oppression and the payer was innocent *Shelley v. Paddock* [1978] 3 All ER 129; Affir'd CA [1980] 1 All ER 1009.

Consequently, according to the civil law, a trader in prohibited goods owns the proceeds he receives. If they are seized without lawful excuse, he can sue for their recovery. In 1910 a street bookie whose takings had been confiscated by the police brought a successful action for their recovery. The court rightly said that if the bookie were denied title his pockets could have been rifled by the first passer-by or even by the constable who arrested him. Whether unlawful proceeds should be confiscated to the state was a matter for the criminal law and the judge who sentenced him.[12]

Between the 'fence' who is discovered with stolen goods and the drug dealer found with his takings there is a grey area where the civil law is more ambivalent as to whether unlawful proceeds can be taken from a wrongdoer. In this area, there are victims whose rights have been infringed and who consequently (unlike the drug purchaser) have a civil cause of action but the loss which the victims have suffered is less than the profit which the defendants have made out of their wrongs. Profit to the culprit exceeds loss to the victim. The question is then posed as to whether the victim should only receive compensation for the loss, or whether the defendant should be made to disgorge the whole of the profit which he has improperly acquired.

The law of contract generally takes the first approach. A contract can normally be broken with impunity to make a more profitable deal elsewhere.[13] The contract-breaker must pay compensation to the innocent party, but he will not have to pay the possibly higher profit which the alternative deal will yield. Economists have praised this principle as encouraging the most efficient use of resources.[14]

(3) Unjust enrichment

It is not always, however, that a civil wrongdoer can keep the profits of his wrongdoing. Under the collective rubric of 'unjust enrichment' there is a number of situations where this is not so. In these situations the defendant has profited from a civil wrong to an extent which exceeds the loss suffered by the plaintiff, but the plaintiff is nevertheless entitled to recover the whole of that profit. Some commentators think that a general principle should evolve from these separate situations.[15]

Of course, when someone has wrongfully deprived another of his

---

12. *Gordon v. Chief Commander of Metropolitan Police* [1910] 2 KB 1080.
13. Treitel, *op cit.*, p. 701.
14. Beale, *Remedies for Breach of Contract* (Sweet & Maxwell, 1980) pp. 160–4; cf. Goff and Jones, *The Law of Restitution* (Sweet & Maxwell, 1978) 2nd edn., p. 371 who advocate allowing the victim of a broken contract a restitutionary remedy to reach the additional profit made by the defendant.
15. See Goff and Jones, *passim* but particularly pp. 469–524.

property the law entitles the wronged individual to recover that property or its value and, if the wrongful deprivation amounts to criminal conduct, the criminal court can itself frequently, by the use of its powers to order restitution (see chapter 7), effect redress without the wronged person having to resort to the civil courts. But this is not remedying an unjust enrichment save in very simple terms; in such cases the wrongdoer's enrichment is exactly matched by the wrongdoer's loss.

In those cases however where, at the instigation and for the benefit of a wronged individual, a wrongdoer is deprived by law of the profit he has made, the remedy provided effectively penalises the wrong committed.[16] These cases are analogous to those for which we recommend powers of confiscation should be given to the Crown, namely cases where there is no, or no identifiable, victim of crime.

Examples of cases where the civil courts have provided plaintiffs with remedies of this type are:

(a) Account of profits from using another's intellectual property

It is an offence to infringe someone's patent, trademark or copyright. The owner can bring a civil claim for compensation for any loss that has been suffered as a result. Alternatively, however, the owner may seek an account of the profits which the defendant has made.[17] If the defendant has had access to markets or opportunities which would have been closed to the plaintiff, these profits may well far exceed the compensation.

(b) Account of profits from abuse of trust[18]

Trustees and other fiduciaries are held to a high standard by the courts. They must account to the beneficiaries or others on whose behalf they act for any profits which they make from abusing the trust or from exploiting opportunities which came to them because of their position. Again, this may be unjust enrichment in the simple sense of restitution (if the opportunity was one which would otherwise have accrued to the beneficiary) but it may be unjust only in the sense of penalising a wrong. In one case[19] a solicitor, who learnt of an invest-

16. Professor P.B.H. Birks, 'Restitution and Wrongs' (1982) *Current Legal Problems* 53.

17. Kerley, *The Law of Trade Marks* (10th edn., 1972), paras 15–80; Copyright Act 1956 sect. 17(3) and *Skone-James on Copyright* (11th edn.) para 573; Patents Act sect. 60 and *Patents for Inventions* (4th edn., 1974) paras 12–127. Michael Crewe, 'Damages and Account of Profits', Auckland University Law Review, pp. 197–208.

18. Goff and Jones, *op. cit.*, pp. 490–511. Equity's willingness to grant an account derived in part from its inability to entertain claims for damages *Re Collie; Ex parte Anderson* (1878) 8 Ch. D. 807, 819.

19. *Boardman v. Phipps* [1967] 2 A.C. 46.

ment opportunity while acting for a trust, took advantage of the opportunity himself and was compelled to account for all the profit that he had made. The trust had known of the opportunity, but had been more cautious and deliberately decided not to pursue it.

(c) Waiver of tort[20]

If a person's goods are wrongly kept or detained by another, the owner can sue for the tort of conversion or wrongful interference with the goods and obtain compensation for the loss he has suffered.[21] If the defendant has used the goods more effectively or profitably than the plaintiff could have done, the law allows the plaintiff to forgo or 'waive' his claim in tort and claim the profits instead.[22]

(d) Exemplary damages[23]

The usual purpose of damages is to compensate the plaintiff for his loss, but there is a persistent strand of judicial opinion that in some cases, at least, damages can be used to punish the defendant and to deter him and others from committing the tort again. The House of Lords[24] has severely curtailed this power to give 'exemplary damages', but it survives (amongst other grounds) where the defendant's conduct was calculated to result in profit.[25] Thus a publisher of a grossly defamatory but highly profitable story has been ordered to pay exemplary damages to reflect its improper gain.[26] So, too, has a landlord who 'winkled out' a sitting tenant by harassment in order to sell his property at a much higher price.[27]

All of these remedies have the effect of confiscating the proceeds of wrongdoing, but they do so by giving the plaintiff a windfall benefit. In each case the plaintiff is better off as a result of the wrong and its

---

20. Goff and Jones, *op. cit.*, pp. 469–85; Daniel Friedmann, 'Restitution of Benefits Obtained through the Appropriation of Property or the Commission of Wrong' (1980) 80 Columbia L.R. 504; Birks, *op. cit.*

21. Torts (Interference with Goods) Act 1977, sect. 3. If the defendant still has the goods, the court has a discretion to order specific delivery with or without the option to pay damages of their value; *ibid.*

22. Apart from conversion, deceit and trespass, it is unclear which torts can be waived. Goff and Jones argue that wherever a tortfeasor has been unjustly enriched (in either sense used in the text) the plaintiff should be able to obtain the benefit by waiver p.472. W.V.H. Rogers argues conversely that the list of waivable torts is now closed, *Winfield and Jolowicz on Tort*, 11th edn. by W.V.H. Rogers (1979), p. 687.

23. H. Street, *The Law of Damages*, pp. 34–6; Ogus, *The Law of Damages* (1973) pp. 27–38; *McGregor on Damages* (14th edn. 1980) pp. 309–34.

24. *Rookes v. Barnard* [1964] A.C. 1129; *Cassell & Co. v. Broome* [1972] A.C. 1027.

25. *Ibid.*

26. *Cassell & Co. v. Broome* (above).

27. *Drane v. Evangelou* [1978] 2 All ER 437, *McReady v. Rum, The Times*, 24 October 1970.

remedy than if he had suffered no interference with his rights at all. They are all, frankly, penal sanctions and as such are thought by some to sit uncomfortably in the civil law system. In Canada it has been said that to award exemplary damages against a defendant who has already been convicted for the same wrong is to inflict a double punishment.[28] In the House of Lords, Lord Devlin justified the remaining categories of exemplary damages as necessary 'to teach wrongdoers that tort does not pay'.[29] Yet he acknowledged that this penalty was imposed without the safeguards that surround other state-imposed punishments.[30] In a criminal case the Crown must prove its case beyond reasonable doubt, a plaintiff has only to show that his version is more likely than not. A criminal defendant can only be cross-examined as to his previous convictions and character in very limited circumstances; a civil defendant, if he gives evidence, can be discredited much more freely. A plaintiff can prove his case by aid of discovery; the Crown cannot compel a defendant to make incriminatory disclosures.[31] A jury acquittal is final, but a civil defendant who wins at the trial level can face a renewed attack on appeal. Those accused of serious crimes have a right to jury trial; very few civil defendants have the same right and those that do can only opt for a jury to determine their liability if they are also willing to take the risk that they might be unsuccessful and that it will then be for the jury to fix the penalty. The Faulks Committee recommended that exemplary damages in defamation actions should be abolished and said.[32]

We do not like the idea of fining a defendant in a civil action and presenting the fine not to the state but to the plaintiff who has already received aggravated compensatory damages for the injury to his feelings and damage to his reputation.

---

28. *Loomis v. Rohan* (1974) 46 DLR (3d) 423 (B.C.S.C.). cf. Street *op. cit.*, p. 34.
29. *Rookes v. Barnard* at pp. 1226–7.
30. *Ibid.*
31. Discovery cannot be used in even a civil suit for the recovery of a penalty. R.S.C. Order 24r.2(3) -2(3). e.g. for double damages against a tenant for fraudulent removal of his chattels to avoid distress Landlord and Tenant Act 1737 sect. 3, *Hobbs v. Hudson* (1890) 5 QBD 232 but a defendant could not object to discovery to a copyright owner who claimed damages for conversion of all infringing copies under sect. 18 of Copyright Act 1956. Though these might far exceed the diminution in the value of the plaintiff's copyright (cf. the level of damages under sect. 17), they were not a penalty. According to Dillon, J. they were, like waiver and constructive trusts 'a form of redress which the courts have worked out as appropriate for a Plaintiff whose rights have been infringed' – *Richmark Camera Services Inc. v. Neilson-Hordell* (1981) FSR 413. As we comment in the text, these are not mutually exclusive categories: rightly or wrongly, the courts have considered a penal remedy appropriate for certain kinds of infringement of rights.
32. *Report of the Committee on Defamation*, Cmnd 5909, para 356.

A similar comment might be made on the other examples which are given above where remedies for unjust enrichment have been developed to penalise the defendant's wrongdoing.[33]

We do not think that the problem of confiscating proceeds of crime should be solved by expanding these remedies.[34] Although, as we noted in chapter 2, private enforcement of the criminal law was once positively encouraged, the establishment of police forces and the institutionalisation of prosecutions have long made this anarchronistic.[35] A further indication of the antipathy to giving civil plaintiffs a 'bounty' is the Protection of Trading Interests Act 1980. US law, for instance under the anti-trust legislation, allows private plaintiffs to recover damages amounting to three times the loss they have suffered. In the 1980 Act Parliament approved a scheme for allowing defendants (at least those who were not resident in the US) a cause of action in England to recover that part of their damages that exceeded the compensatory element.[36]

While we do not favour expanding the powers of the civil courts to order confiscation, their experience is useful in several respects in considering the nature and extent of the powers that might be given to the criminal courts.

(a) The means of the defendant

In calculating compensatory damages, the court takes no account of the defendant's means; the plaintiff's entitlement to compensation exists independently of the defendant's ability to pay. Exemplary damages, however, are different. Because of their penal nature, the means of the defendant are relevant.[37] The issue has not been discussed (as far as we are aware) in the context of the other remedies referred to above. In any powers of confiscation which may be given to the criminal courts we believe that, they being penal in nature, the means of the defendant should be a relevant consideration.

(b) Unlawful savings

One variant of the civil remedies considered above is to make the defendant pay a reasonable fee for the property which he appropriated

---

33. Cf. the comments in Prosser, *Torts*, 3rd edn., p. 73, as to waiver.
34. Contrast Grodecki 71 LQR 254; Higgins 25 MLR 149; Sabbath 8 ICLQ 486, 689.
35. A number of statutes once gave the informant whose evidence led to a conviction a right to a reward to be taken from the defendant. These were all repealed by the Common Informers Act 1951.
36. Protection of Trading Interests Act 1980 sect. 6.
37. *Rookes v. Barnard* [1964] AC 1129 at p. 1228.

or the opportunities which he wrongfully exploited.[38] Similarly, a person who wrongfully detains goods can be made to pay compensation for each day he kept the goods, although the owner could not have let them out or otherwise used them profitably for the whole of that time.[39] In each case the defendant is made to account for costs which he improperly tried to avoid. It makes sense to treat such 'negative benefits' similarly to positive benefits. Where the civil law has tried to distinguish the two (as with waiver)[40] it has attracted powerful criticism.[41] We feel that a new criminal power would be subject to criticism of equal force if it treated the negative benefit of unlawful cost-cutting differently from the positive benefits of an illegal sale. For example, the extra profit made on the lawful sale of a house from which a sitting tenant has been unlawfully winkled is no less the proceeds of crime than the payment for illegal drugs.

(c) Calculating profits[42]

The ease with which this can be done varies greatly. It is most difficult where the profit was due in part to legitimate efforts and in part to unlawful methods.[43] Even here, as in the case of a house sold with vacant possession rather than with a sitting tenant, it may be relatively easy. The development of economic theory and accounting methods may make the exercise rather easier than when Lord Cottenham had to struggle with the then novel concept of marginal cost in calculating how much the Derby Gas Light Co. had saved by using gas meters which infringed the plaintiff's patent. He gave up in despair and recommended that the parties settle.[44]

Deducting expenses is one method of calculating the defendant's gain. It still leaves open the issue as to what expenses are to be deductible. The marginal cost approach which baffled Lord Cottenham has been adopted in some American cases so that the defendant could deduct such items as salesmen's salaries and expenses in selling

---

38. For example, *Wrotham Park Estates Co v. Parkside Homes Ltd* [1974] 2 All ER 321, 339 *et seq.* where a defendant who profited by infringing a restrictive covenant was ordered to pay damages on the basis of the reasonable fee which the covenantee could have charged for waiving the covenant; *Telex Corp. v. IMB* 367 F. Supp. 259 (U.S. Dist. N.D. Okla. 1973) rev'd in part 510 F2d 894 (10th Cir. 1975) Where Telex saved computer development costs by poaching IBM employees and exploiting their confidential information.
39. *Strand Electric and Engineering Co. Ltd v. Brisford Entertainments Ltd* [1952] 2 Q.B. 246 C.A.
40. *Phillips v. Homfray* (1883) 24 Ch. D. 439.
41. See the dissenting judgment of Bagally, J. in *Phillips v. Homfray*; Goff and Jones, *op. cit* at p. 476; *Edwards v. Lee's Administrators* 96 S.W. 2d 1028 (1936).
42. See G.B. Klippert *Unjust Enrichment* (Butterworths, Toronto, 1983) pp. 215–32.
43. *Siddell v. Vickers* (1982) 9 R.P.C. 152, 162 per Lindley L.J.
44. *Crosley v. The Derby Gas Light Co.* (1838) 3 My & Cr. 428; 40 ER 992. Cf. a similar plea by Slade, J. in *My Kinda Town v. Soll* [1982] FSR 147, 158.

their copy of the plaintiff's gin but not the insurance premiums and real estate taxes which they would have had to bear in any event.[45] Overhead expenses have been taken into account in other cases, particularly (and perhaps ironically) where the wrongful acts have taken up a substantial part of the defendant's business.[46] Where the defendants or their employees have legitimately contributed to the product's success it would be over-generous to the plaintiffs to award them the whole of the net profit even after deduction of whatever expenses are appropriate. Consequently in one US case where the defendant plagiarised the plaintiff's play and turned it into a movie film, although the plaintiff's copyright had been infringed, the profitability of the film was attributed to the director, cast and production as well as to the script. The plaintiff was awarded 20% of net profits.[47]

A third approach to calculating profits is to make the defendants pay costs which they have avoided or side-stepped by wrongful means. This has been considered above.

Mathematical exactness is often an impossibility and the courts are usually satisfied with a reasonable approximation based on expert testimony.[48] As Lord Shaw once said the judges must be guided by 'the exercise of a sound imagination and the practice of the broad axe'.[49] The burden of proof is critical and it probably rests with the defendant to show which part of his profits were lawfully made.[50] It is interesting to note that the Australian and New Zealand drugs legislation similarly places this burden on the defendant.[51]

(d) Forfeiture

Deodand (see chapter 2) was an early form of forfeiture which did not depend on a criminal conviction. Since its abolition in 1846 there are relatively few situations in which property closely associated with a crime can be forfeited by administrative act or civil process. Those that there are should more properly in our view be characterised as quasi-criminal and accordingly have been considered in chapter 8.

---

45. *Century Distilling Co. v. Continental Distilling Corp.* 205 F2d. 140 (3rd Cir. 1953).
46. *W.E. Bassett and Co. v. Revlon Inc.* 435 F2d 656 (2nd Cir. 1970).
47. *Sheldon v. MGM* 309 US 390 (1940).
48. *Sheldon v. MGM; Watson Laidlaw & Co. Ltd v. Pott Cassels and Williamson* (1914) 31 RPC 104, 114.
49. *Watson Laidlaw* at p. 118.
50. *Peter Pan Manufacturing Corporation v. Corsets Silhouette Ltd* [1963] 3 All ER 402, though in *My Kinda Town v. Soll* Slade, J. thought the burden lay on neither party. *Ibid.*, p. 158.
51. Misuse of Drugs Amendment Act 1978 sect. 42 (N.Z.); Customs Act 1901 sect. 243 c(4) as added by Customs Amendment Act 1979 (Commonwealth).

4 Confiscation in other jurisdictions

(1) The United States

Before 1970[1]
The American colonists regarded feudal forfeiture as part of the *ancien régime* which their War of Independence was intended to overthrow. The US Constitution forbade corruption of the blood and forfeiture of estate for treason except during the traitor's lifetime.[2] The first Federal Congress abolished forfeiture and corruption of the blood for felony.[3]

There was not the same dislike of specific statutory forfeitures and customs and revenue legislation was quickly introduced to adopt these powers.[4] In the main these, like the comparable English provisions (see chapter 6), did not depend on a criminal conviction but could be imposed or declared in civil proceedings. An important question has been whether the 'civil' classification of the proceedings meant that the procedural rights guaranteed by the US constitution to those charged with a criminal offence were inapplicable. The US Supreme Court answered in 1827 that owners of forfeited property did not have the same rights as those charged with a criminal offence, at least where the proceedings were analogous to the forfeiture proceedings by the Revenue and Customs authorities in the English Court of Exchequer or Admiralty. In those cases the property itself was treated as the offender 'as the guilty instrument or thing to which forfeiture attaches' (the proceedings were thus described as '*in rem*') and policy considerations were used to justify its imposition despite the innocence of the owners.[5] But the US courts also recognised that this personification theory could, if not checked, rapidly subvert the constitutional guarantees of a fair criminal trial. The Supreme Court, therefore, insisted that it should be limited to cases where possession of the forfeited property was itself an offence, or where the property

---

1. For this section we have relied heavily on James Maxeiner, 'Bane of American Forfeitures Law – Banished at Last?' (1977) 62 Cornell Law Review 768.
2. Art III S 3 cl. 2.
3. I Stat 117 (1790) now 18 U.S.C. 3563.
4. Maxeiner, pp. 779–81.
5. *The Palmyra* 25 U.S. (12 Wheat) 1 (1827); *U.S. v. Brig Malek Adhel* 43 U.S. (2 How) 210 (1844).

was subjected to some unlawful use or put into some unlawful condition. Forfeiture proceedings *in rem* could not be used if they depended on proof of the owner's guilt of a criminal offence.[6]

This stand was undermined by the Civil War. Many confederates owned property which was in the area controlled by the Federal Government. They could not be brought to face a criminal trial for obvious reasons. Congress therefore proposed to forfeit their property. President Lincoln considered vetoing the bill on the grounds that forfeiture would depend on a finding that the owner was guilty of treason and was obnoxious because the owner would not have the constitutionally required procedural rights. However, when Congress compromised on other disputed issues, he relented. The Act was later upheld by the Supreme Court as an exercise of the war-making power.[7]

The precedent of punitive forfeiture was followed after the civil war. The anti-trust legislation of 1890, for instance, enacted forfeiture proceedings[8] as one method of enforcement. Although these could not be justified as part of a war effort, they were nonetheless upheld by the Supreme Court. The Court did insist, at first, that these punitive *in rem* suits be attended by at least some of the rights of a criminal trial. Searches and seizures had to conform to the Fourth Amendment to the Constitution and self-incriminating evidence could not be compelled without violating the Fifth Amendment.[9] These requirements have been retained and, since US law will not allow evidence to be used in a criminal trial that has been obtained in breach of the constitutional provisions, such evidence is also excluded from *in rem* forfeiture proceedings.[10]

However, in other respects the courts have rolled back the procedural restrictions on punitive forfeiture. It is, for instance, no longer a bar to such actions that the owner has been acquitted by a criminal court, not does collateral estoppel apply to stop relitigation of similar issues.[11] Finally, beginning with a case in 1921,[12] the Supreme Court has established that *in rem* forfeiture may be used to deprive a person

6. Maxeiner, pp. 784–5; *Miller v. U.S.* 78 U.S. (11 Wall. 268, 321 (1871 in dissent); The Amy Warwick 1 F. Cas. 808, 811 (D. Mass. 1862) aff'd 67 U.S. (2Black) 635 (1863).

7. Maxeiner, pp. 786–7; *Tyler v. Defrees* 78 U.S. (11 Wall) 331.

8. Sherman Anti-Trust Act 1890 s6, 15 U.S.C. 6.

9. *Boyd v. U.S.* 116 U.S. 616 (1886); cf. *Coffey v. U.S.* 116 U.S. 436 (1886) – double jeopardy prohibition contravened forfeiture proceedings following on acquittal.

10. *U.S. v. $537285 in U.S. Coin & Currency* 91 S.Ct. 1041 (1971) *One 1958 Plymouth Sedan v. The Commonwealth of Pennsylvania* 85 S.Ct. 1246.

11. For example, *One Lot Emerald Uncut Stones and One Ring v. U.S.* 93 S.Ct. 489 (1972) reversing *Coffey* (see above) and holding that an acquittal in criminal proceedings is neither a bar to *in rem* forfeiture nor creates an issue estoppel.

12. *Goldsmith-Grant v. U.S.* 254 U.S. 505 (1921).

of his property though he had no knowledge of its unlawful use and had done everything within his power to prevent it so being used. For instance under a Puerto Rican statute a boat rental company was deprived of a yacht that it had rented out because the hirers of the boat were found to have had one marijuana cigarette with them. The hire contract forbade hirers to use such drugs and the owners knew nothing of the breach of this term. Nonetheless applying the personification theory the Supreme Court held the boat to be guilty and the owners' innocence irrelevant.[13]

'Civil' forfeiture and confiscation relating to drug offences

It will thus be seen that legislatures in the US have been much more ready to allow forfeiture of property involved in criminal activities without the need for a criminal trial. In American terminology, these are 'civil' forfeitures, because such challenges as can be made are brought in the civil courts. In our view this is a misnomer: a penalty is quite clearly being imposed on the owners of the property and the holders of an interest in it. We deal with this theme in chapter 12. For the sake of consistency with our American sources, we will in this section adopt the American terminology and refer to this type of forfeiture as 'civil'.

In 1970, Congress passed the Psychotropic Controlled Substances Act ('the CSA').[14] This allowed the federal government to forfeit five categories of property connected with drug offences. These correspond approximately to the types of property that are commonly forfeited in the UK under sect. 27 of the Misuse of Drugs Act 1971 (though again we stress that in the UK forfeiture of this kind only follows conviction). Thus they include the drugs themselves,[15] the equipment, products and raw materials,[16] containers for forfeitable drugs,[17] any conveyances used or intended for use in or facilitating the transportation, sale, receipt, possession or concealment of forfeitable drugs[18] and records kept by drug violators.[19]

More significantly for our purposes, in 1978 Congress added as a sixth category the proceeds of illegal drug sales and of money intended to be used to purchase prohibited drugs. The new section provided that the following could be forfeited:

---

13. *Calero-Toledo v. Pearson Yacht Leasing Co.* 416 U.S. 663 (1974).
14. 21 U.S.C. 881.
15. 21 U.S.C. 881 (a) (1) 21 U.S.C. 881 (f) & (g).
16. 21 U.S.C. 881 (g) (2).
17. 21 U.S.C. 881 (a) (3).
18. 21 U.S.C. 881 (a) (4).
19. 21 U.S.C. 881 (a) (5).

All moneys, negotiable instruments, securities or other things of value furnished or intended to be furnished by any person in exchange for a controlled substance in violation of . . . [the CSA]

all proceeds traceable to such an exchange

all moneys, negotiable instruments and securities used or intended to be used to facilitate any violation of [the CSA]

Except that no property shall be forfeited under this paragraph to the extent of the interest of an owner by reason of any act or omission established by the court, to have been committed or omitted without the knowledge or consent of that owner.[20]

The first and third paragraphs again correspond approximately to the types of property that can be forfeited by a UK criminal court under the Misuse of Drugs Act 1971 or under sect. 43 of the Powers of Criminal Courts Act 1973. The second paragraph, however, has no present English correlation; in our terms it is a power of 'confiscation'.

There have been few decisions so far on the type of property that can be taken as 'proceeds traceable to such an exchange', but the Department of Justice clearly anticipates that the courts will use the concepts and rules of tracing as developed in the civil law of restitution.[21]

The Department also argues that all categories of property that are forfeitable under the Controlled Substances Act become the property of the US Government from the moment of their illegal use.[22] As we shall see, this has significance primarily for those who later acquire the property. Formal forfeiture proceedings are still necessary to declare the government's rights. As with the pre-1970 specific statutory powers of forfeiture these are *in rem* proceedings. In the case of personal property, jurisdiction depends on the property having been seized; in the case of land, it depends on the constructive possession of posting notices on the land. All seizures, including those for forfeiture purposes, are only constitutional under the Fourth Amendment to the US Constitution, if the government has probable cause. The US courts are divided on whether the Controlled Substances Act requires the government to satisfy a magistrate in advance of the seizure that probable cause exists and to obtain a warrant.[23]

The procedure for challenging the legality of the forfeiture after seizure depends on the value of the property: over $10,000 the matter

20. 21 U.S.C. 881 (a) (6).
21. Myers and Brozostowski, 'Drug Agent's Guide to Forfeiture of Assets' Drug Enforcement Administration (Washington D.C., 1981) pp. 142–57.
22. *Ibid.*, pp. 205–7.
23. *Ibid.*, p. 182.

is adjudicated upon in the civil courts, which in the federal system means by a judge and jury. Below $10,000, the matter is dealt with administratively; that is, it is determined by an attorney from the Washington Office of the Department of Justice. By posting a bond for $250, a complainant can elevate administrative into judicial proceedings.[24] It may come as no surprise that a significant number of forfeitures are appraised at a value of just over $9000 but under $10,000.[25]

In whichever procedure is followed the government must begin by showing that the property is *prima facie* subject to forfeiture. If it succeeds the complainant has the burden of proving that the property was wrongly taken. Few complainants have been able to do this. The categories are broad and may involve proving that another person did not have a criminal intention, for instance in the case of a car intended for use in transporting unlawful drugs. Most importantly, the personal innocence of the complainant, even if established to the satisfaction of the tribunal, is not generally sufficient to overturn the forfeiture.[26] (For the special case of 'proceeds', see below.) As has already been observed, *in rem* forfeitures proceed on the fiction that they depend on the guilt of the property rather than its owner. Further the statute provides that the 'property' itself is forfeit, i.e. all rights in the property and not merely the interest held by any wrongdoer: consequently a complainant cannot succeed by showing title paramount and non-involvement in the offence.[27] Finally, because the property is deemed to be forfeit at the time it is illegally used or the intention to use it illegally is formed, successors in title, even though bona fide purchasers, have no better claim to it than the wrongdoer.

Three very narrow defences mitigate the position. A complainant is entitled to recover property that was stolen from him and only later involved in drug dealing. Second, a common carrier's conveyance is not subject to forfeiture, although used to carry contraband unless the carrier knowingly acquiesced.[28] Third, as can be seen from the quotation above, the 'proceeds' and 'purchase price' category added in 1978 has a particular defence for bona fide owners.

The legal position of innocent owners of property is not therefore strong. They can, however, petition the Department of Justice to exercise its discretionary powers of remission or mitigation.[29]

24. 21 U.S.C. 881 (d).
25. Steven Zimmerman, *Symposium of the Canadian Federal/Provincial Task Force on Enterprise Crime* (1982).
26. *Calero-Toledo v. Pearson Yacht & Leasing Co.* above note 13.
27. *Ibid.*
28. 21 U.S.C. 881.
29. 21 U.S.C. 881 (d).

Property is remitted if it is returned to the petitioner without conditions. It is mitigated if it is returned subject to payment of some financial penalty. These powers are widely used. Between 1976 and 1979, for example, the Drug Enforcement Administration and the Customs Service (under various civil statutes related to criminal activity most closely associated with drug trafficking) seized and disposed of $161 million. All but $29.9 million, or 18.5%, was returned under the remission or mitigation powers. (Not all of this will have been to innocent owners, because mitigation is used, like compounding by the English customs authorities, where the violation is relatively minor and can be adequately dealt with by a small fine.)[30]

Criminal forfeiture and organised crime

In 1970 the US Congress incorporated forfeiture into two further measures. Both the Racketeering Influenced Corrupt Organisations Act, or RICO[31], and the Continuing Criminal Enterprise Offence, or CCE[32], are attempts to deal with massive and pervasive organised crime.

(i) The triggering offences RICO and CCE resemble sect. 43 of the UK's Powers of Criminal Courts Act 1973 in that all require a conviction as a pre-condition of forfeiture. In US terminology they are all therefore 'criminal' forfeitures which are applied after *in personam* proceedings against a particular defendant. However, unlike the English provisions which can be used in any serious case, the American criminal forfeitures are limited to specified offences, indeed to offences that are also created by the statutes themselves.

The RICO offence requires proof that the defendant has committed a 'pattern of racketeering', which means at least two specified serious offences, and that the racketeering has been connected in some way with an 'enterprise'. There is a sufficient connection if the enterprise was used to carry out the racketeering, was acquired illegally by racketeering or legitimately with the proceeds of racketeering offences.

The CCE is aimed more specifically at drug trafficking. It strikes at the leaders of a group of five or more associates who commit a federal drug offence as part of a continuing series (three or more) of such offences and from which they obtain substantial income or resources.

The model of creating new offences as a predicate for forfeiture is

30. *Asset-Forfeiture – A Seldom Used Tool in Combatting Drug Trafficking*, Report of Comptroller General to Senator Joseph Bidden (Washington, D.C., 1981).
31. 18 U.S.C. 1962, 1963.
32. 21 U.S.C. 848: part of the Controlled Substances Act which also allowed for civil forfeiture; see p. 32 above.

not particularly attractive for the United Kingdom. The US Statutes were reactions to a problem of organised crime and drug trafficking on a very large scale. Britain has both, but not on the same scale. Second, the model had a particular purpose within a federal structure. All of the specified 'racketeering' offences were crimes already, but generally under state statutes. RICO gave the federal courts jurisdiction. There is no comparable need for new offences in our unitary system. Third, they reflect an enthusiasm for charging conspiracy or similar offences which is not presently shared in the UK.

Consequently, it is not proposed to examine or evaluate the triggering offences,[33] but rather to look at the forfeiture consequences which are of more relevance in considering changes for the UK.

(ii) The forfeiture provisions Both RICO and CCE impose mandatory forfeiture on conviction.[34] In both cases the defendant loses his interest in the enterprise. He also forfeits 'any interest in, security of, claim against, or property of or contractual right of any kind affording a source of influence over' the enterprise. Under this provision corporate and union officials have been deprived of their offices.[35]

The legislative intention in the case of RICO seems to have been not as simple as depriving a wrongdoer of his illegal profits; rather it was to separate the offender and his corrupting influence from legitimate businesses.[36] Unlike the CCE,[37] RICO gives no express power to forfeit profits which the defendant has received from the enterprise and the courts have said that the legislative purpose of 'cleansing' the enterprise of the defendant's influence did not enable this further power to be added to the racketeering statute by implication.[38] However, in a significant decision, a court held that the forfeiture provisions applied equally to a defendant's interest in a wholly illegal

---

33. See Blakey and Goldstock, 'On the Waterfront: RICO and Labor Racketeering' (1980) 17 Am. Crim. L.R. 341; W.L. Schmidt, 'RICO: An Analysis of the Confusion in its Application and a Proposal for Reform' (1980) 33 Vand. L.R. 441; Blakey and Gittings, 'RICO' Basic Concepts – Civil and Criminal Remedies' (1980) 53 Temp. L.Q. 1009.

34. *U.S. v. L.'Hoste* 609 F2d 796 (5th Cir. C.A. 1980).

35. For example, *U.S. v. Rubin* 559 F2d 975 (5th Cir. 1977). When Governor Mandel of Maryland was convicted under RICO the court refused to declare his governorship forfeit. It baulked at describing the state as an 'enterprise': *U.S. v. Mandel* (see below).

36. William Taylor, 'Forfeiture under 18 USC 1963 – RICO's most Powerful Weapon' (1980) 17 Am. Crim L.R. 379, 383–5.

37. 'Any person who is convicted [of an offence under the CCE provision] shall forfeit to the U.S. . . . .
    (a) The profits obtained by him in the enterprise.'

38. *U.S. v. Thevis* 474 F. Supp. 134 (1979).

enterprise.[39] This suggests that the courts may be moving away from viewing RICO as a cleansing agent and more towards regarding it as a power of confiscation. There have been proposals to amend the legislation to make this clear.[40]

(iii) Third party rights[41]

We saw that in the case of 'civil' forfeiture, third party rights were infrequently recognised. They are accorded more respect in the case of criminal forfeiture.

It is only the defendant's interest which is forfeitable. Consequently, if the defendant has no interest, the property is immune. In the context of companies, this has meant the court deciding whether a third party is the beneficial owner of shares or whether in reality he holds them for the defendant.[42] Because only the defendant's interest is forfeited, lessors, mortgagees and lienholders are also protected. They have a legal right to prevent forfeiture of their interest, not merely the opportunity to petition the Attorney-General for remission or mitigation.

Rather more difficulty has been experienced where the defendant is a co-owner. In one case, for instance, the defendant's wife objected to forfeiture. They lived in a state where property acquired after the marriage belonged to them jointly. The court, although accepting her innocence for the sake of argument, nonetheless ordered forfeiture. It thought that the Attorney-General (who has the same powers of remission and mitigation as in the case of civil forfeiture) could make any necessary adjustment.[43] A rather more satisfactory reason for reaching the same conclusion has been suggested.[44] This is that although the property was jointly owned, both partners had power without reference to the other to dispose of it voluntarily. Since each bore the risk of the other dissipating their communal assets, each had also to accept that the other might subject the property to forfeiture.

Similar difficulties have been experienced in deciding the rights of

---

39. *U.S. v. Turkette* 101 S.Ct. 2524 (1981); *U.S. v. Maruben American Corp.* 611 F2d. 763 (1980).
40. *Asset-Forfeiture*, for example.
41. See generally, Bruce Warren, 'RICO Forfeitures and the Rights of Innocent Third Parties' (1982) 18 Cal. Western Law Review 345.
42. For example, in *U.S. v. Mandel* (see note 50) where the jury decided that a third party who apparently owned a race track was really a nominee for the defendant. An appellate court struck down the forfeiture order because the third party had had no opportunity to be heard. This should presumably have been granted after the defendant's conviction, though the burden of proof and the status of the jury's verdict would have been problematic. Taylor, *op. cit.*, p. 396.
43. *U.S. v. L'Hoste.*
44. By Warren, *op. cit.*

those to whom part of the enterprise or other forfeitable property has been transferred after the illegal activity. The Department of Justice has argued that criminal forfeiture, like civil forfeiture, takes effect at the moment the unlawful act is committed and that the judgment of the court is simply declaratory of rights which have already accrued. The defendant on this basis has no title after using the property in an illegal way which he can confer on even a *bona fide* purchaser. The latter's only recourse is to petition the Attorney-General.[45] At least one court has refused to accept this argument.[46] It has said that criminal forfeiture can only affect a person who has been convicted; third parties to whom forfeitable property has been transferred cannot suffer unless they are also prosecuted. Further, since the aim of RICO is to 'cleanse' the enterprise of its corrupt influence, the government should be unconcerned once control has passed to innocent successors.

RICO says little about how these third party claims are to be resolved other than to apply the civil forfeiture procedures under the customs law 'with such modifications as are necessary'. Because of the basic difference between forfeiture of the entire property (under civil forfeiture) and forfeiture of only the defendant's interest (under RICO) these modifications will have to be considerable.[47]

(iv) Procedure

a. *Indictment*   Forfeiture proceedings under these two statutes are *in personam*: they depend on the defendant rather than on the property being before the court. US law requires the prosecution to give adequate notice to the defendant of its intention to seek forfeiture and due process in resolving the issue of liability to forfeiture. These two aims are met by including in the indictment a separate count which specifies the property and the defendant's interest which is alleged to be forfeitable.[48] After conviction, the jury is then requested to bring back a special verdict on this count.

b. *Pre-trial seizure*   In many cases it is recognised that, if no action were taken to preserve the status quo until judgment on this final count, the forfeitable property would disappear. RICO and CCE therefore provide express powers for pre-trial restraining orders and

---

45. Myers and Brozostowski, 'Drug Agent's Guide to Forfeiture of Assets', p. 330.
46. *U.S. v. Thevis.*
47. *Asset-Forfeiture.*
48. Federal Rules of Criminal Procedure Rule 31(e) Rule 7 (c) (a).
49. 18 U.S.C. 1963 (b) and 21 U.S.C. 848 (d).

performance bonds.[49] However, the US courts[50] have been sensitive to the prejudicial effect of such orders on a defendant awaiting trial and have required the government to show: (a) that it is likely to be able to convince a jury that the defendant is guilty beyond reasonable doubt; (b) the defendant will otherwise dispose of the property; (c) third party rights will not be harmed; and (d) such an order is in the public interest.

US prosecutors complain that the first requirement is unreasonable because it requires them to disclose their case prematurely. In federal criminal procedure the prosecution is not required to give details of its case to the defence before trial. It frequently does so as a matter of practice, but the residual discretion, particularly in cases of the kind that will be prosecuted under RICO, is regarded as important.[51] There could not be the same objection in the UK, for in an indictable case the Crown will anyway have to prepare statements for the committal proceedings setting out its full case. Nevertheless, there is almost invariably a delay of some weeks between arrest and the completion of these statements.

As an alternative to using these powers, some prosecutors have used civil forfeiture to seize property pending the criminal trial.

c. *Substitution of assets* In at least three situations, the question has been raised as to whether untainted assets can be forfeited. The first is where the defendant has exchanged the forfeitable property for something else. Although there have been few judicial decisions (reflecting perhaps the difficulty of proving the necessary links in the chain), it is assumed that, as in the civil law, the government can 'trace' its property into these substitutes.

The second situation is where the defendant offers to pay a monetary penalty instead of forfeiting his assets. This can be advantageous both to the defendant and to the government. In one case the asset was

---

50. *U.S. v. Mandel* 408 F Supp. 679 (D.Md 1976) 591 F2d. 1347 (4th Cir.) reversed on other grounds 602 F2d 653 (2nd Cir. 1979) in which case a restraining order was refused because it would have been 'substantially prejudicial' to the defendants. Contrast *U.S. v. Bello* 470 F. Supp. 723 (S.D. Cal. 1979) which criticised *Mandel* as emasculating the power to grant restraining orders. It denied *Mandel's* conclusion that a pre-trial order would entail an impermissible pre-trial finding of guilt and decided that the grand jury's decision to return the indictment was sufficient evidence of probable cause. This argument has been described as 'unpersuasive' because of the *ex parte* character of grand jury decisions and the absence of power to review the sufficiency of evidence to support the indictment. Barry Tarlow 'Rico: The New Darling of the Prosecutor's Nursery' (1980) 49 Fordham Law Rev. 165, 298. Tarlow would consider there to be no fundamental unfairness if the *ex parte* restraining order were of short duration and was followed by an *inter partes* hearing with the right to cross-examine witnesses (p. 299).

51. Cf. Tarlow above, p. 305.

the defendant's house and the arrangement allowed his family to remain in their home and the government was spared the trouble and expense of appraising, preserving and selling property. The courts have been prepared to countenance this type of substitution (known as 'buy-back') with the caveat that, in the case of RICO prosecutions, it should not be used so as to leave the defendant in control of the enterprise from which forfeiture was intended to purge him.[52]

The third situation is where forfeitable assets can be identified, but they are outside the jurisdiction. The government has proposed that it should then be able to forfeit 'clean' assets within the jurisdiction. There is no indication that this is possible under the present statute but an amendment to allow this has been suggested.[53]

d. *Disposal of property*   RICO and CCE (and the civil forfeiture powers) have resulted in the government acquiring a diverse range of types of property. Appraising, safeguarding and disposing of them has presented administrative problems which are still being resolved.

Effectiveness of RICO and CCE

Until 1980, the powers of criminal forfeiture were used relatively rarely. In this first decade only $1,964,000 was forfeited.[54] Part of the explanation is the complexity of RICO and CCE offences which were seen by many prosecutors as simply duplicative of existing offences handled by state prosecutors. The courts had also warned prosecutors of the dangers of abuse where RICO was invoked outside its intended context of organised crime.[55] Perhaps more fundamentally though, forfeitures following criminal convictions were unknown between 1790 and 1970. Prosecutors had no experience of them and gave them little thought. In 1981, the Comptroller-General in a report to the US Senate criticised prosecutors for not realising the potential of forfeiture.[56]

The lesson for England seems to be that if similar new powers are introduced, they will have only marginal importance unless the police and prosecution authorities are trained to consider them and to assemble the evidence necessary to show what property is forfeitable. The elusiveness of such evidence has been a further problem in RICO's effectiveness.

52. 'The RICO Statute: An Overview' Research Divison of the Secretariat of the Solicitor-General of Canada p. 29; cf. Taylor *op. cit*; pp. 396–7 who questions whether 'buy-backs' are compatible with RICO's purpose of cleansing legitimate organisations.
53. *Asset-Forfeiture*.
54. *Ibid*.
55. *U.S. v. Huber* 603 F 2d (2nd Cir. 1979) p. 395.
56. *Asset-Forfeiture*.

It is also worth observing that forfeiture does not appear to lead to shorter prison sentences. Rather it has been seen as an additional penalty.[57]

(2) Australia

In 1979, the Commonwealth of Australia enacted a procedure for assessing penalties on those suspected of involvement in illegal drug trafficking.[58] The legislation is detailed and illustrates many of the issues that we have considered in relation to a new confiscation power in England.

It is firstly a power limited to drug offences. In part this may be a reflection of the Commonwealth government's limited constitutional powers, in part of the particular concern which is felt for drug trafficking. In this latter respect, it is similar to the Hong Kong Bribery Ordinance.[59] Both make use of procedures and presumptions which are in sharp contrast to the customary methods of punishing those suspected of criminal offences.

Like 'civil' forfeiture in the US the Australian powers are not dependent on a conviction or pending prosecution. However, whereas American civil forfeiture proceeds are *in rem* (against property which has been identified and seized), the purpose of the Australian process is to fix a pecuniary penalty which is a personal obligation. This penalty is an attempt to assess 'the value of the benefits derived by the defendant by reason of his having engaged in . . . prescribed narcotics dealings'.[60] The statute emphasises that the Court's task is to assess gross benefits; any expense or outgoings are to be disregarded. The revenue may be from a single transaction or over the period that the defendant can be shown to have engaged in the drug trade. In calculating income over a period the Court must presume that any increase in the value of the defendant's property over the same time was attributable to his unlawful activities unless he can prove otherwise.[61]

Although the Court's task is to calculate in monetary terms the defendant's revenue, it is also given the power to direct an official receiver to take control of all or part of the defendant's property.[62] The government can apply *ex parte* for such an order if it can produce affidavit evidence to show reasonable grounds for believing that the defendant committed the offence and has derived benefits from it.

---

57. *Ibid.*
58. Customs Amendment Act 1979 (Cwlth) – amending Customs Act 1901 – the following references are to the 1901 Act as amended unless otherwise specified.
59. Prevention of Bribery Ordinance sect. 12(3) Cap 201, Laws of Hong Kong.
60. (Aust) 1901 Act sect. 243B(2).
61. S.243C(2) (e), (3).
62. S.243E.

These orders resemble English *Mareva* injunctions referred to in chapter 9 except that control of the property is vested in a receiver. Like Mareva injunctions, the Australian orders can allow the defendant to meet reasonable living and business expenses. Like them, too, they can also be made conditional on the Government giving an appropriate undertaking to pay costs or damages.

Mareva injunctions, as chapter 9 shows, can include an order that the defendants swear an affidavit as to the whereabouts of their assets. The Australian legislation gives the Federal Court a similar power.[63] It can also summon the defendant to be examined by a judge or a registrar on the same issue.[64] Answers given in such an examination cannot be used against the defendant except in assessing the pecuniary penalty or as part of a perjury prosecution.[65] The immunity apparently does not extend to answers given on affidavit and so is narrower than the comparable privilege in relation to discovery in civil intellectual property cases conferred by sect. 72 of the English Supreme Court Act 1981.

Ownership of the property subject to an Australian order is not ordinarily vested in the receiver. Rather the Commonwealth government has a charge over the property.[66] The charge is postponed to any earlier charge or encumbrance and can be defeated by even a later purchaser who was *bona fide* and gave value.

Before the receiver can transfer the detained property or its proceeds to the government, he must obtain a second order from the court.[67] If this is made within six months of the presentation of a bankruptcy petition, the government's proprietary right is further circumscribed. It must then return any part of the payment it has received and rank as an unsecured creditor.[68] Thus while the interests of such creditors are not taken into account in calculating the pecuniary penalty, they are considered in its enforcement.[69]

(3)   Other countries
Civil law countries, and particularly those with penal codes based on those of France or Germany, have for many years had provisions simply allowing or requiring a court to confiscate the product or profit

63. S.243F(1) (d).
64. S.243F(1) (e).
65. S.243F (3).
66. S.243J.
67. S.243G.
68. S.243L.
69. The Australian law was reviewed by Stewart, J. in the Commonwealth's Royal Commission of Inquiry into Drug Trafficking (Canberra 1983).

of an offence.[70] These general powers usually exclude (i) offences of negligence or strict liability; (ii) 'contraventions' or regulatory offences, though other statutes may remove the exclusion and allow confiscation for specific infringements. The general power is usually confined to property that belongs to the perpetrator, though some countries will permit confiscation unless the third parties can establish their *bona fides*.[71] Some countries specifically address the issue of compensation and provide that 'in the absence of other assets, victims may look to the confiscated assets for their indemnity'.[72]

70. For example Belgian Penal Code (1867) Art. 42; Danish Penal Code (1930) Art. 77; Finnish Penal Code (1889) Art. 16; German Penal Code Arts. 73 & 74; Criminal Law Applicable to Greenland (1954) Art. 113; Greek Penal Code (1950) Art. 76; Dutch Penal Code (1886) Art. 33; Icelandic Penal Code (1940) Art. 69; Italian Penal Code (1930) Art. 40; Lebanese Penal Code (1956) Art. 69; Luxembourg Penal Code (1879) Art. 42; Norwegian Penal Code (1902) Arts. 34 and 36; Spanish Penal Code (1944) Art. 48; Turkish Penal Code (1926) Art. 36; Yugoslav Penal Code (1948) Art. 62A.
71. For example, Italy, above.
72. For example, Iceland, above.

Part Two

5 Compensation

The present position
There are three ways in which the victim of a crime may obtain
compensation for the injury, pain and suffering he has sustained. The
criminal court which tries the offender may order him to pay compensation. Second, if the victim suffered personal injury, he may apply
for compensation to the Criminal Injuries Compensation Board (the
CICB). Last, as most crimes also amount to civil injuries, he may
pursue his remedy through the civil courts.

A victim who obtains an order for compensation from the criminal
court is thereby deprived neither of his right to make a claim for
compensation from the Criminal Injuries Compensation Board nor to
pursue his civil remedy. Of course, in either case, any compensation
received as a result of an order by the criminal court has to be taken
into account in assessing the amount to be paid by an award of the
CICB or by the judgment of a civil court.

(a) Compensation orders
The statutory powers of the courts to award compensation are very
wide. Compensation may be ordered for any personal injury, loss or
damage resulting from the offence for which the defendant is convicted or any other offence taken into consideration (Powers of
Criminal Courts Act 1973 sect. 35(1)). Both the Crown Court and
magistrates can order compensation. The courts have discouraged any
attempt to evade the payment of compensation by the introduction of
concepts of causation which apply to the assessment of damages in the
law of contract or tort. They have held that whenever the making of
an order for compensation is appropriate, the Court must ask itself
whether loss or damage can fairly be said to have resulted to anyone
from the offence for which the defendant has been convicted.[1]

(b) Statutory restrictions
The 1973 Act places some restrictions on this general power to award
compensation:

---

1. *R v. Thompson Holidays Ltd* [1974] 1 QB 592.

(1) An award cannot be based on loss suffered by the dependants of a victim of crime.[2]

(2) Compensation cannot be awarded for loss, injury or damage due to a road traffic offence unless the damage resulted from a traffic offence which was an offence under the Theft Act 1968.[3]

(3) The defendant's means must be taken into account in making an award of compensation.[4]

(4) Compensation orders made by magistrates may not exceed a statutory limit.[5]

Until recently a further statutory restriction existed. An order could only be made in addition to some other penalty.[6] Bentham's philosophy that compensation embodies 'the two great ends of justice' (see chapter 1) was taken a stage further in 1982 when Parliament removed this requirement: a compensation order can now be the sole measure imposed upon an offender.[7] Compensation orders are in addition now given priority over fines.[8]

Three of these legislative restrictions need no further discussion at this stage. A few words must however be added about the defendant's means.

(c) The defendant's means

The methods available to enforce compensation orders emphasise the fact that they answer both of Bentham's aims of justice: punishment as well as compensation. Consequently, it is right that while civil judgments are generally awarded irrespective of the debtor's ability to pay,[9] compensation orders should take account of the defendant's means.[10] The Court of Appeal has said that orders can properly be made although they call for some sacrifice or extra effort on the part of the offender, but they should not be made where defendants have no assets, no employment and no prospect of a job.[11] The Court said in one case, 'Compensation orders were intended as a convenient and

2. Sect. 35(3).
3. *Ibid.*
4. Sect. 35(4).
5. Magistrates Courts Act 1980, sect. 40.
6. Powers of Criminal Courts Act 1973, sect. 35(1).
7. Criminal Justice Act 1982, sect. 67(a) substituting a new s (1) in sect. 35 of the 1973 Act.
8. *Ibid.*, sect. 67(b) adding sect. 35 (4A) to the 1973 Act.
9. This statement must be qualified by the court's important jurisdiction to restructure the obligations of a debtor under a regulated consumer credit agreement to take account of the defendant's means. Consumer Credit Act 1974, sect. 129(2) (a), 130.
10. 1973 Act sect. 35(4).
11. *R v. Bradburn* (1973) 57 Cr. App. R. 948; *R v. Oddy* [1974] 2 All ER 666.

rapid means of avoiding the expense of civil litigation when the criminal clearly has the means to pay.'[12] Compensation orders, like fines, can be made payable in instalments, but where the instalments would have to be paid over more than two years the orders have generally not been approved.[13]

The obligation to take into account the defendant's means and the undesirability of leaving a debt over the defendant's head for a long time are reasons why the courts have generally struck down compensation orders against those who are given, or who are already serving, an immediate custodial sentence unless they have savings or an assured job on their release.[14] The Widgery Sub-committee (of the Advisory Council on the Penal System) whose recommendation led to the present power to order compensation disapproved of coupling such orders with imprisonment unless the sentence was short or the defendant had savings.[15] The ineffectiveness of combining a compensation order with loss of liberty was borne out by a small study in London of 27 orders made by a crown court at the same time as an immediate custodial sentence.[16] In over half there had been no payment at all after three years (in comparison with one-tenth of magistrates' compensation orders generally).[17] and in eight more there had been only partial payment. Of a total of £9426 ordered only £1782 had been actually paid and half of this had been taken from defendants on their arrest.

(d) The 'clear case' restriction
The courts have, in addition, placed one very limiting restriction upon the exercise of the power. The 'general principle' which emerged from the discussion in the Widgery Sub-committee was that 'criminal courts cannot be expected to make any kind of detailed assessment of the extent of the victim's loss and that it is only in straightforward cases that the criminal courts can order reparation'.[18] Although the legislation itself places no such restriction upon the exercise of the

12. *R v. Inwood* (1974) 60 Cr. App. R. 70; cf. *R v. Daly* [1974] 1 WLR 133. See generally Rodney Brazier Appellate Attitudes towards Compensation Orders' [1977] Crim. L.R. 710.

13. *R v. Making* (1982) 4 Cr. App. R(S) 180 *R v. Carole Anne Hunt* (9 December 1982) [1983] Crim. L.R. 270.

14. For example, *R v. Wylie* [1975]R.T.R. 94.

15. Sub-Committee (chaired by Lord Widgery) Report 'Reparation by the Offender' (1970) paras 124 and 137; the view was reiterated in the Advisory Council's Report 'Maximum Sentences of Imprisonment' (1978) para 290.

16. Softley and Tarling, 'Compensation Orders and Custodial Sentences' [1977] Crim. L.R. 720.

17. Softley, 'Compensation Orders in Magistrates Courts' Home Office Research Unit Study no. 43 (1978) p. 24 (based on figures for a week in 1974).

18. Widgery Sub-Committee Report para 81.

power to award compensation the courts have followed the sub-committee's lead. In a number of cases, the Court of Appeal has held that a criminal court should only impose compensation orders in 'clear' cases.[19] We consider this further below. The majority of us feel that the reasons for this limitation in the case of convictions in the Crown Court are purely matters of expediency; they have no basis in principle. In the magistrates' courts the limitation as to amount is justifiable on the ground that magistrates have little experience in determining civil liability, but no such justification is present in the case of crown court judges.

(e) The Criminal Injuries Compensation Board

The Criminal Injuries Compensation Board makes payments out of government grant-in-aid to those who have suffered personal injury directly attributable to a crime of violence or to an attempt to arrest a suspected offender or to prevent an offence. If the victim died, a claim may be made by a spouse or dependant. To qualify for an award an applicant's injuries must attract compensation of at least £400 (£500 in the case of family violence). The incident must normally have resulted in criminal proceedings or been reported to the police without delay. Claimants must assist the Board, for instance by providing any relevant information requested. Compensation will not be paid where the injury arose out of a road traffic offence, unless the vehicle was deliberately used to cause harm, or where the victim and offender were living in the same family unless, in the case of adults, they separated permanently after the offence. The Board will look to see if the victim was responsible for the offence; provocation, particularly in the case of a sexual offence, may preclude compensation. Applications must normally be made within three years.[20]

Compensation is calculated on common law principles but with additional limitations. There is a maximum for lost earnings and no exemplary damages are paid. A claim can be reduced or refused if 'having regard to the conduct of the applicant, before, during and after the events giving rise to the claim, and to his character and way of life or, in application in fatal cases, to the conduct, character and way of life of the deceased or the applicant it is inappropriate that he should be granted a full award or any award at all should be granted'.[21]

19. For example, *R. v. Kneeshaw* [1975] Q.B. 57. C.A.; *R v. Thompson Holidays* [1974] 1 Q.B. 592.
20. Criminal Injuries Compensation Scheme. See the Board's 19th Report for 1982/3, Cmnd 9093, 1983, Appendix E, paras 4–8. The increase in the minimum threshold to £400 was announced with other changes in February 1983. These are set out in Appendix F.
21. *Ibid.*, paras 12, 6(c).

In 1982/3 £29 million was paid out. While the Board deducts from the award or recovers from the applicant any compensation paid under an order of a criminal court in respect of injuries for which it makes an award, this has a negligible effect on its income. In 1982/3, for instance, the Board received only £142,740 as a result of such orders.[22]

(f) Compensation and civil proceedings

The advantages of a compensation order over civil remedies are plain. The determination of liability is made more quickly and is obtained at no expense to the victim. Further, if the defendant does not pay the order, more severe and effective methods of enforcement can be used than against civil debtors. So, for instance, money found on defendants at the time of arrest, or on their person in court, can be used to satisfy the debt. Those who refuse to pay compensation orders ultimately can be sent to prison; recalcitrant civil debtors cannot.[23] Another advantage is that a conviction is conclusive of liability in a criminal court; in a civil court evidence of a conviction, if relevant, is admissible but rebuttable.[24]

(2)   The use made of the available remedies

Compensation orders have proved to be very popular with sentencers, but they have been used unevenly. In 1982 compensation orders were made by magistrates against 64% of offenders causing criminal damage. By comparison, compensation was ordered against only 17% of offenders convicted of violence against the person.[25] The difficulties of assessing a proper figure for the victim's loss are obviously greater in the case of personal injury, and magistrates are conscious that the CICB can award compensation for more serious cases. Guidelines for suitable amounts for pain, suffering and inconvenience have been published by the Council of the Magistrates' Association.[26].

The reason why some sentencers seem hesitant to award compensation for personal injury may, at least to some extent lie in victims'

---

22. See 1983 Report, para 41.
23. Magistrates Courts Act 1980 sect. 76, 80 For crown courts see Administration of Justice Act 1970 sect. 41 (as amended by Criminal Law Act 1977 Sched. 13). The Court ordering compensation can stipulate a period of imprisonment in default, but this power is to be used sparingly *R v. Bunce* (1977) 66 Crim. App. R. 109. Imprisonment for debt was abolished except for tax and maintenance defaulters by Administration of Justice Act 1970 sect. 11 Sched. 4 following the recommendation of the Payne Committee (Enforcement of Judgment Debts) Cmnd 3909, 1969.
24. Civil Evidence Act 1968 sect. 11 (see chapter 3 note 8).
25. *Criminal Statistics England and Wales* , Cmnd 9048; cf. J. Vennard, 'Magistrates Assessments of Compensation for Injury' [1979] Crim. L.R. 510.
26. See *The Magistrate*, 10 October 1980, p. 156.

ignorance of their rights. So far as we know the only research on the subject was carried out by Dr Joanna Shapland and others in 1978–9. It was limited both numerically and geographically but, so far as it went, it revealed in two reports (the last of which was in December 1982) some disturbing findings. In two Midlands cities 278 victims of violent crime were interviewed. Of these 218 were asked about compensation after the outcome of the case. Two to three years later those who had applied to the CICB or who had benefited from compensation orders made by criminal courts were reinterviewed.

(1) Only 34% applied for either kind of compensation but only 35% said they did not want compensation (7% were doubtful). Most of those who wanted compensation named small sums, below the then (in 1978) CICB minimum of £150.

(2) 51% did not know of any source of compensation. Only 18% knew about compensation orders, and only 39% about the CICB. Victims in one city seemed better informed than those in the other, chiefly because more knew about the CICB for some reason. Although the sizes of the samples are only moderate, the probability that the difference was attributable to chance is less than 1 in 40. Most of those who knew about compensation orders or the CICB applied for compensation.

(3) Most of the knowledgeable victims were police officers. 'It was extremely rare for any victim other than a police officer (and not all of them) to have anything other than a vague awareness of the possibility of existence of some compensation body prior to victimisation.' Of the 84 victims who knew about the CICB 40% were told by police who were 'on the case', another 20% by colleagues or friends in the police, and 7% by Citizens Advice Bureaux or law centres.

(4) Of the 55 victims who applied to the CICB, 82% got compensation. Since the sample was small, other samples would be likely to yield percentages ranging from about 70% to about 93%. 91 victims who would have liked compensation did *not* apply to the CICB. Only 20 of these got it from the courts (the report does not apparently indicate how many applied to the courts).

(5) 'Except in . . . not guilty trials, victims are rarely informed or able to discover when the relevant court appearance is to take place.'

(6) The information given to the court about the victims' injuries or losses seems to have been very incomplete. '. . . in some cases no details of injuries suffered were cited at all in court.'[27]

27. The report is unpublished as yet, but the references on the typescript are as follows: p. 7; pp. 10, 11, 13; p. 21; pp. 22 and 24; p. 46; pp. 47ff.

The position may be very different in other parts of the country and it is fair to record that we did not specifically consult on this question. However, a member of our committee, Deputy Assistant Commissioner Sewell, has been able to give us some information, so far as the area covered by the Metropolitan Police is concerned, which paints a more satisfactory picture. In 1982 the Metropolitan Police assisted in the presentation of 5,296 claims to the Criminal Injuries Compensation Board, and this figure was substantially exceeded in 1983. CICB leaflets are handed to victims by the police and, at any rate in the Metropolitan area, victims are informed of the trial date, even when it is known that there is going to be a guilty plea. Dr Shapland's findings, however, are evidence that there are cities in which the system for giving victims such information is not as effective in practice as in theory. So far as paragraph (6) above is concerned the details of injury, often supported by photographs, will be in the depositions and, if no details are given to the Court, then that can only result from a failure by the prosecution to draw the Court's attention to them.

(3) The defendant's means

We have no doubt whatever that it is proper for the Court to take into account the defendant's means when making an order for compensation.

Most defendants come from the lower income groups and, particularly in times of recession and unemployment their means have been eroded. Our committee received evidence of the inability of some courts to appreciate the poverty and hardship of many people living on supplementary benefit and the financial incapacity to meet compensation orders, even by quite modest instalments.[28] We are also aware of cases where defendants have exaggerated their means (e.g. by pretending to be still in a job which they have lost as a result of the criminal proceedings) in order to give a better impression to the sentencer, and especially in order to avoid being sent to prison. Since means assessment is a procedural issue which is common to many of the themes of this book, we return to it in chapter 11.

There is one further addition to the powers of the court which we think should be given. The objections to combining a compensation order with a sentence of imprisonment do not apply in a case when a sentence of imprisonment is suspended. An offender is not thereby prevented from earning his livelihood. However, the same problems do arise if the suspended sentence is activated. At present there is, in such circumstances, no power to vary a compensation order (unless, fortuitously, the original sentence is still subject to appeal).[29] We

28. Owen Wells of the National Association of Probation Officers.
29. *R. v. Whenman* [1977] Crim. L.R. 450 C.A.; cf. D.A. Thomas's comment.

think the Court ought to have the power to vary or extinguish the order in the light of the defendant's changed circumstances.

(4) Limitations on the court's powers

The evident advantages from the victim's point of view of a compensation order obtained at, or as a result of, a criminal trial make it desirable that as few limitations as possible be placed upon the exercise of the power. We turn now therefore to consider the various limitations, legislative, judicial and practical, to which we have briefly referred. We do so in that order. Because the legislative restriction in respect of road traffic offences is justified on the ground that, because of insurance, most victims will not have to bear the loss themselves, we take the opportunity at that stage of our report of considering the whole question of the interaction between compensation and insurance.

(a) Dependants of a deceased victim

The Powers of Criminal Courts Act 1973 does not allow the court to award compensation to the dependants of a victim for the loss which they have suffered.[30] This limitation resulted from the recommendation of the Widgery Sub-Committee which dealt with this question summarily:

> The power should not in our view extend to compensation of dependants of victims who die as a result of the injury. At common law no civil claim arises out of causing death because the victim is not available, and liability in fatal cases is the artificial creation of statute based on loss to the deceased's dependants. We think that claims of this kind are quite unsuitable for consideration by a criminal court.[31]

This reasoning does not appeal to us as sufficient justification for this limitation. Undoubtedly, until new procedures are provided, some dependants' claims are likely to be too complex to satisfy the 'clear case' requirement. However damages for bereavement are currently fixed at £3500 by statute[32] so that there is no difficulty whatever in making that assessment, nor would there be any problems of complexity to prevent the court making an award of that sum or, in view of the defendant's means, a lesser sum, in a proper case. In our view this restriction should be removed. We hope that procedures can be devised to enable even complex cases to be adjudicated upon in those rare cases where the offender's means justify an award.

(b) Road traffic offences and the relevance of insurance

Loss that arises out of the presence of a motor car on the road cannot

30. 1973 Act sect. 35(3).
31. Widgery Sub-committee Report, para 51.
32. Administration of Justice Act 1982 sect. 3.

be the subject of a compensation order unless it results from an offence under the Theft Act 1968 (such as theft or taking and driving away a motor vehicle without permission).[33]

One justification given for this exception is that most victims will not have to bear their loss themselves: they will either be covered by insurance or indemnified by the Motor Insurers' Bureau (though it covers only personal injury and not property damage).[34] The relevance of insurance in the making of compensation orders is of general importance. It is an issue on which our committee was divided.

Some of our members regarded insurance as irrelevant.[35] In the first place, even insured persons could suffer financially: a no claims bonus might be lost or the insurer might otherwise fix the premium for renewal of the policy at a higher level, and any claim involves a certain amount of time and inconvenience. In any event, insurance is a matter of private agreement between the victim and the insurance company; the victim pays for his benefits by premiums and should not be prejudiced by this. Civil claims can be pursued for the benefit of insurers, and so, too, should applications for compensation orders. To deny insurers their right of subrogation in civil claims or their ability to benefit from criminal compensation orders might increase the cost of insurance. Alternatively, to restrict compensation to those who were not insured might be a disincentive to insure. Further, some large companies 'self-insure' and spread their loss by adjusting the price structure for all their goods or services. Would they, too, be barred from receiving compensation? At the practical level, it would be difficult for criminal courts adequately to test the ability of a victim to recoup loss from insurance or elsewhere. The Court would more frequently want the victim to give evidence, and this would lengthen the proceedings, particularly in the case of guilty pleas when victims currently often do not attend court. Finally, those who oppose taking cognisance of insurance or risk-spreading ability point to the value of compensation orders in linking offenders' punishment to the loss they have caused. It is irrelevant for these purposes that the loss has been suffered by an insurer or other large company.

Those of our members[36] who think that insured losses should not be the subject of compensation orders emphasised the fact that com-

---

33. Powers of Criminal Courts Act 1973 sect. 35(3).
34. Widgery Sub-committee Report, para 63.
35. Sir Derek Hodgson, Sir Christopher Staughton, J.M. Sewell, Louis Blom-Cooper, Tony Leifer, Professor Walker, Martin Iredale.
36. Andrew Nicol and Clive Soley.

pensation orders are an additional remedy to civil proceedings for damages. In comparison with civil remedies, it is a quicker and cheaper remedy and backed by imprisonment if not obeyed. These advantages should only accrue to victims who would otherwise suffer hardship or bear the loss themselves. The use of this additional remedy is not justified where victims are indemnified by an insurer or otherwise able to spread their loss. The likelihood of criminally caused loss being made good by a compensation order is quite low. It is unlikely to influence many people in their decision whether to insure or not. Similarly, the general level of premiums are unlikely to be affected. Subrogation is beyond the Committee's terms of reference, but it is noted that it has not escaped critical comment. As Professor Atiyah has said, 'it is confidently suggested that any serious study of the problem must lead inevitably to the conclusion that subrogation, far from being a device which ought to be extended should, on the contrary, generally be confined within the narrowest possible limits and, in most cases, abolished altogether'.[37] This part of our membership recognise that the opportunity for reparation would be diminished but think that where the victim was a corporation, neither guilt nor atonement is likely to be experienced in the same degree. Unrecouped loss, such as deductibles, or increased premiums could consistently, with this view, be made the subject of compensation.[38]

Aside from insurance the road traffic exception largely overlaps with the 'clear case' requirement; that is, the issues of contributory negligence, liability and quantum would frequently be too complex to be dealt with quickly at the end of a criminal trial. However where the loss and liability are clear it is illogical to prevent the courts from ordering compensation. The 'exception to the exception' of Theft Act offences makes the anomaly worse, as *Quigley v. Stokes* demonstrated.[39] There a joy-rider was involved in a collision. The owner of

37. Atiyah, *Accidents Compensation and the Law*, 3rd edn. (Weidenfeld and Nicolson, 1980), p. 457. Atiyah observes that where subrogation is exercised against an individual tortfeasor it has the effect of shifting liability from an organisation with the ability to spread loss (the insurer) to a person who must bear the loss himself or herself, i.e. the reverse of the modern 'risk allocation' theory of tort liability. Further, insurers seem ready to forgo their claim to subrogation against individuals. Motor insurers commonly agree to bear the loss of their insured's vehicle 'the knock for knock' agreement, which precludes subrogation. The V & G Insurance company's refusal to participate in such schemes was described as one of the major contributions to its collapse by the subsequent inquiry. Again employers' liability insurers have eschewed their right to seek subrogation from the negligent employees. In Scandinavian countries subrogation against an individual tortfeasor has been limited or abolished by statute. *Ibid.*, pp. 454 and 652.

38. Legislation would need to make clear that insurers were not entitled to claim this as part compensation for their loss.

39. [1977] 2 All ER 317.

the car that had been taken could recover compensation because his loss resulted from the unlawful taking and driving away. The owner of the other car could not, because that damage was caused 'only' by the joy-rider's careless driving. The illogicality can be justified only by convenience. Since road traffic offences take up such a high proportion of summary proceedings, it would greatly increase the workload of magistrates' courts even to consider the suitability of a compensation order.

(c) Compensation orders by magistrates for personal injury

The guidelines published by the Council of the Magistrates' Association are well below the levels that would be awarded for comparable injuries in a civil court. This was the view not only of those of our members who themselves know what these levels are but also of the Chairman of the CICB which handles more claims for personal injury than do all high court and county court judges combined.[40]

It is our view that guidelines should be given to magistrates, but that they should emanate from some source with greater knowledge of the 'going rate' in the civil courts than the magistrates' own association possesses or has the means to possess. We also think that the guidelines should be reviewed and amended annually. The Chairman of the CICB thought that his Board, the members of which all have great experience in these matters, could devise more appropriate guidelines. We agree, particularly as the two methods of compensating a victim are so closely linked, the lowest current limit of the CICB providing a line below which a compensation order is most obviously desirable if it can be made. If the CICB were prepared to provide guidelines and look at them at regular intervals we think that this would be of great benefit.

(d) The 'clear case' requirement

As we have said the reasons given for the Court's imposition of the clear case restriction on the power to grant compensation are all matters of expediency, not of principle. They stem largely from the present deplorable back-log of cases awaiting trial and this is entirely understandable. We would not want the implementation of any of the recommendations which we make to extend the already unreasonable delay faced by those on remand in custody or on bail awaiting trial, and that would, no doubt, be the immediate effect of any substantial extension of the number of cases in which the courts were called upon to consider questions of compensation.

The problems connected with reducing the back-log of criminal

---

40. The Board received over 29,000 applications and resolved 26,000 in 1982/3. 19th Report, Cmnd 9093, para 2.

cases awaiting trial are not our concern, but we believe it would be defeatist to restrict our recommendations to those that would be acceptable only in the present situation. We can but hope that the present state of the criminal lists will not be allowed to persist for long.

We are however not impressed by the various ways in which it has been sought to clothe expediency with the mantle of principle. It is said that compensation orders must be limited to clear cases because there is no available procedure which would enable a criminal court to make a compensation order in a difficult or complicated case. There are no pleadings and no provision for discovery of documents or facts. That is the present position, but it does overlook the fact that liability would already have been decided against the defendant upon a far more stringent test than the balance of probabilities which is the criterion for liability in a civil court. The only, though in some cases no doubt complicated, questions that would remain would, in the vast majority of cases, relate only to assessment of the damage suffered. There will, no doubt, be the rare case where, although the defendant is guilty of criminal conduct and the victim has thereby suffered loss, questions of contributory negligence or causation arise. We see no reason why a judge in the crown court should not normally deal with such questions. Nothing we say should be implied as suggesting any different principles for testing whether a claim for compensation has been made out. If it were thought necessary in cases where particularly difficult questions of compensation could be foreseen as possibilities the case could be allotted to a high court or nominated circuit judge or recorder. That would be no more than a very limited extension of the present practice where specified categories of case are restricted to trial either by a high court judge or, on release, to specified circuit judges. And, in the long run, we doubt whether there would be any additional use of court time. Assuming the victim has a good case for compensation and the offender the means to pay, pursuit of the remedy in the civil courts will be more lengthy, more costly and more wasteful of court time than if an award could be made at the same time as guilt is decided.

So far as the relative inexperience of magistrates is given as a reason for limiting the award of compensation to clear cases we think that the statutory limitation as to amount largely looks after this difficulty.

In our view, while we appreciate the practical difficulties which would, in present conditions, follow any increase in the number of cases where a court was required to consider matters of compensation we believe that steps should be taken to achieve this end.[41]

41. Andrew Nicol and Clive Soley take a different view. See their Note of Dissent, page 144.

(5) Practice and procedure

The present practice is devised within the context of the 'clear case' principle. However, sect. 67 of Criminal Justice Act 1982 points the way forward by providing that courts should make compensation orders 'of such amount as [they] consider appropriate, having regard to any evidence and to any representations made by or on behalf of the accused or the prosecutor'.

It is standard practice in some police forces to elicit from complainants information about the nature and value of their loss.[42] This can then be presented to the Court by the police or prosecution if the defendant is convicted. It is not essential for the victim to apply in person for compensation because an order can be made 'on application or otherwise'.[43] This is particularly useful where a defendant has given advance notice of an intention to plead guilty and the victim would not therefore be needed as a trial witness. In Scotland it is now the duty of the prosecutor to send the victim a leaflet explaining how to seek compensation.

However, in *R v. Vivian* (1979)[44] the Court of Appeal insisted that before a compensation order could be made the amount of the loss had to be formally proved if it was not agreed by the defendant. In that case, prosecuting counsel had told the court that the owner of a motor car had received a repair estimate of £209 for damage done by the defendant, a joy-rider. The defendant claimed this was excessive. The judge made a compensation order of £100, which was quashed by the Court of Appeal who ruled that since even this amount had been neither agreed nor proved by proper evidence the order was improper. Sect. 67 of the Criminal Justice Act 1982 was intended to reverse this narrowing of the Court's powers and to allow the Court to have regard to any evidence and to any representations made by the parties. *R v. Cornwell*[45] is an example of how an admission can be the basis of a compensation order.[45] The defendant admitted stealing stock worth £6000 from a wholesaler. The victim showed that over the same period £8600 of stock had disappeared. The sentencer (perhaps splitting the difference) had ordered compensation of £7300. The Court of Appeal agreed that other causes might have accounted for some of the stock losses and the only safe premise was the defendant's admission. It substituted an order to pay £6000. In a later case,[46] the Court ruled that *Vivian* had no application to small sums of compensation for

42. For example, Metropolitan Police Standing Orders para 206A(5).
43. 1973 Act. sect. 35(1).
44. [1979] 1 All ER 48.
45. (1979) 1 Cr. App. R. (S)19.
46. *Bond v. Chief Constable of Kent* [1983] 1 All ER 456.

personal injury or shock or suffering and it allowed an order for £25 to stand against youths who had thrown stones at a house window and terrified the occupants.

In a civil suit, receipts, estimates and reports would be disclosed to the defendant well before the trial. We think a similar practice should be adopted with similar documents used to support a claim for compensation. It is only fair that the defendants should know that claims for compensation will be made, have them particularised and have the opportunity to consult experts of their own to judge their reasonableness. If defendants are presented with these details for the first time after conviction and while sentence is being considered, they could, of course ask for an adjournment, but both the Court and they might be reluctant to postpone the sentencing decision, especially if social inquiry reports have already been prepared and there is no other cause for delay.

The increasing popularity of compensation may in part be due to the police practice of eliciting details of loss referred to above. We realise that this would entail a shift in the role of the prosecution in a criminal trial. In *R v. Johnston*[47] the Court of Appeal had to consider a case where a defendant had been sentenced to four years' imprisonment and ordered to pay £12,000 compensation. The Court, on evidence not available to the trial judge, varied the compensation order to £500. In so deciding the Court held that although the 1973 Act provides that the Court should have regard to the means of the offender so far as they appear or are known to the Court, that did not mean that a burden was laid on the prosecution to establish the defendant's means. The court held that, compensation being a matter of sentence, the prosecution could have no interest in it except, so far as it is customary to do so, to pass on a request from the loser that a compensation order be made. Our own view is that, in the interest of victims of crime, prosecuting authorities should be required to take a much more active part in matters both of compensation and, as we comment later, of confiscation.

We agree that it ought not to be part of the prosecution's role to ask for a more punitive sentence, but where as in the case of compensation, confiscation, restitution or forfeiture there is a dispute about the factual basis on which an order should be made, the prosecutor ought to play a much more active role. The Criminal Justice Act 1982 sect. 67 gives indirect approval to this in the case of compensation by saying that the court must base its decision *inter alia* on representations made by the prosecution. This approach is also consistent with a more general trend, endorsed by the Court of Appeal, of a trial judge

47. [1982] Criminal Law Review, p. 537.

hearing after a plea of guilty or a conviction evidence and argument as to the degree of the defendant's complicity.[48]

The Association of Chief Police Officers, the Justice Clerks' Society and the Magistrates' Association would favour the further step of requiring a sentencing court to consider whether a compensation order was appropriate. We agree that this would be desirable. In particular, it might increase the number of occasions where a small sum of compensation is ordered for offences causing personal injury. It might also increase the use of compensation in preference to fines. On the other hand, compensation should not be foisted on a complainant unwillingly. We agree with the National Association of Probation Officers that an informed waiver by the victim should debar the court from making an order.

The Widgery Sub-committee considered that criminal bankruptcy would provide a means of compensating victims in more complex cases. We consider criminal bankruptcy and its lack of success in chapter 10, but its comparative failure makes it, in our view, necessary to devise some more sophisticated procedures to deal with really complex cases so that all victims of crime shall have equal rights against offenders. Because liability in a criminal case will be decided by the verdict of guilty, these procedures, in the main, will have to be concerned only with quantification and, in rare cases, causation. We see no reason why in cases where the defendant's apparent means make the procedure worthwhile the prosecution should not serve on the defendant in the form of a statement of claim the details of the victim's loss, together with such vouchers as are necessary to substantiate it. If and when the defendant is convicted he will then be in a position to contest the claim in further proceedings before the same trial judge. As we have pointed out this would, in the long run, save in court time by making unnecessary further civil proceedings.

There is another side of the coin which makes it necessary in our view that better procedures for pursuing claims for compensation should be provided. Sympathy for the victim should not blind the courts to the possibility of inflated claims. Evidence we received from the National Association of Probation Officers suggested that these are unfortunately not uncommon.

There is another reason why a victim should be entitled to waive his right to a compensation order from the criminal court. In cases of personal injury where a compensation order is made the victim can seek to make up any shortfall in his proper compensation by making

---

48. *R v. Gortat & Pirog* [1973] Crim. L.R. 648; *R v. Hastie, The Times,* 9 March 1983 – breach of probation order. See generally Sallon, 'Contesting Facts in Pleas in Mitigation' [1983] LAG Bull. 64.

application to the Criminal Injuries Compensation Board. However there will be cases when the criminal court has to make a calculation as to the total amount of a victim's economic loss in order to set an upper limit above which no order can be made. In such cases it seems right that that calculation when made should be binding between victim and defendant. The Court may not order the victim to pay the whole amount, and the victim would then, as he is now, be entitled to pursue a further claim in the civil court but, in any such proceedings, we are of opinion that the assessment of total loss made by the Crown Court should be binding on the parties. The defendant would, of course, have already had a right of appeal but the victim would not, so it is right that the victim should, if he so wishes, forgo the speedy procedures of the criminal court rather than risk an assessment from which he would have no appeal.

6 Matters relating to the making of compensation orders

We turn now to consider a number of matters related to the making of compensation orders.

(a) Should orders be limited to cases where the defendant is civilly liable?
There are crimes that cause clear loss though the victim has no right to damages. Offences under the Trade Descriptions Act 1968, for instance, give no private remedy and while in some cases there may be parallel civil liability on the contract of sale or for misrepresentation this will not invariably be so.[49] Another example is the offence of selling a car in an unroadworthy condition contrary to the Road Traffic Act 1972 sect. 60(3). If the car was sold by the defendant in the course of business, the victim would have a civil action for breach of the implied terms of merchantability or fitness for purpose, but there would be no civil liability if the defendant sold the car privately.[50] In our view, the Court of Appeal rightly said that since compensation orders are intended to short-circuit the procedures of the civil

---

49. The Criminal Justice Bill of 1972 which broadened compensation powers was amended at its report stage to remove the requirement that compensation be for damage to or loss of *property*. This was done in response to Opposition proposals to allow magistrates to give compensation where there had been a breach of the Trade Descriptions Act 1968. Hansard, H.C. 15 June 1972, col. 1924 *et seq*. However the effect of the amendment appears merely to allow compensation for non-physical loss, such as pecuniary loss, suffered for instance by false trade descriptions which are also a misrepresentation or breach of contract. There is no clear indication that the amendment was intended to allow the criminal courts to make an order in circumstances where there would be no civil liability; cf. 'Review of the Trade Descriptions Act 1968' Cmnd 6628, 1976.
50. *Badham v. Lambs Ltd* [1946] 1 K.B.45 also held that there was no civil liability in these circumstances for breach of statutory duty.

system, they ought not to be used where that system would provide no remedy.[51]

(b) Multiple offenders and conspiracy

In the civil law those who jointly commit a wrong are jointly liable for the whole of the loss that they cause. This does not mean that plaintiffs can obtain compensation several times over, but it does mean that they are protected if one of the defendants is unwilling or unable to pay. Compensation orders can in theory similarly be made against each of several offenders for the whole of the loss, but the Court of Appeal has, rightly in our view, said that this is generally undesirable. The amount that each offender pays would then vary according to how much the others have paid rather than according to their means or to their relative culpability. In addition the method by which civil law enables full-paying defendants to recover a contribution from their defaulting colleagues is too clumsy and too expensive for the sums that would normally be involved in adjusting the rights of co-offenders. We, therefore, agree that it is preferable for the sentencing court normally to divide the total amount into *pro rata* shares.[52] The allocation between the defendants can properly be uneven if this reflects their different degree of culpability.[53]

If several defendants are suspected of involvement in an offence they may be charged with conspiracy. It will be recalled that one reason the House of Lords gave in *Cuthbertson* for ruling that the trial judge had no power to confiscate the proceeds of the drug sales was that a conspiracy was not an offence 'under' the Misuse of Drugs Act and so sect. 27 which depended on this pre-condition could not be invoked. Sect. 35 of the 1973 Act is differently worded. Compensation is payable for loss 'resulting from' the offence. Consequently, the Court of Appeal has said that if loss can be shown to have resulted from a conspiracy, it may be the subject of a compensation order.[54] We would agree with this, but not if, as in one case, the defendant is also acquitted of the substantive offence. Again we think it right that a handler can be made to pay compensation to the owner of stolen goods; the handler ought not to be able to argue that the owner's loss was caused by the original theft.[55] The civil law has come to a similar conclusion in regarding each act inconsistent with the owner's title as giving rise to a fresh action in conversion or for wrongful interference with the goods.

51. *R v. Inwood* (1974) p. 73; cf. Atiyah, 'Compensation Orders and Civil Liability' [1979] Crim. L.R. 504.
52. *R v. Grundy and Moorhouse* [1974] 1 WLR 139.
53. *R v. Amey and James* [1983] 1 All ER 865 C.A.
54. *R v. Gleaves* [1977] April 21 (unreported).
55. *R v. Anthony Howell* (1978) 66 Cr. App. R. 179.

(7) A compensation fund?

One motive behind the introduction of compensation orders has been to humanise the criminal justice system by recognising the loss suffered by the victim in some way other than by imposing a stiffer retributive sentence. It was a response to a frequently heard complaint that the criminal process focused on the defendant to the exclusion of the victim. It was also a partial recognition of the fact that a large proportion of victims, like offenders, are poor; they are often people who have no or inadequate insurance and for whom the loss of, or damage to, personal property means real hardship.

Support schemes have expanded rapidly and assist victims to overcome the psychological trauma, but they have few resources to help with financial loss. The Criminal Injuries Compensation Board provides aid for the victims of more serious violence, but can give no help with property damage or small personal injuries. Victims might obtain supplementary benefit such as exceptional needs payment for lost clothing, but not for items regarded as luxuries such as a damaged or stolen television set. It is in the gap between these other schemes that compensation orders are particularly important. However, they are deficient because they are dependent on the person responsible being apprehended and because the offender will often lack the means to pay compensation.

One way of evening out these discrepancies would be to establish a Victims' Compensation Fund.[56] Into this would be paid compensation from offenders, fines and the proceeds of forfeitures and of any new powers of confiscation (see chapter 6). Claims could then be considered irrespective of whether the responsible offenders were caught and independently of their means. Payment could be quicker and in one lump sum rather than spread over instalments as at present. This would in effect be an expansion of the Criminal Injuries Compensation Board which, as noted above, has obtained considerable experience in assessing and dealing with claims from victims of personal violence.

The advantages of such a scheme would not just accrue to individual victims. It would, we believe, extend the humanising influence and concern for victims which were mentioned above. If this more supportive attitude towards victims can be extended, more people might be more sympathetic towards a penal policy which does not tip all our social, economic and emotional problems into prisons.

The obstacles to such a scheme are finance and administration. The

56. We are grateful to Martin Wasik of the University of Manchester for an illuminating paper which he submitted to us and which elaborated on his article, 'The Place of Compensation in the Penal System' [1978] Crim. L.R. 599.

present Chairman of the CICB candidly told us that he thought these would be insuperable and that certainly, his Board could not cope with the volume of work which it would generate without substantial restructuring. As for cost, it is uncertain how much extra revenue confiscation orders would produce and the diversion of fines from their present allocation to the Consolidated Fund would be a form of subsidy. There was also the moral objection that the interposition of such a fund would break the link which a compensation order at present creates between offenders and their victims: payment to a fund would seem no more to be reparation than payment of a fine.

One way of lowering the additional cost and administrative charges would be to confine payments to victims whose defendants had been caught, convicted and ordered to pay compensation and then to the amount of the order. The victim would receive a sum paid at once rather than in a series of instalments which might or might not be completed. The subsidy element would be limited to the underwriting of these risks. It is a more modest and therefore more realistic scheme, but it may justifiably be said to discriminate in favour of victims whose offenders (a) were caught and (b) had sufficient means for a compensation order to be made. These may seem irrelevant criteria for deciding who should benefit but as things are at present many victims anyway have no hope of compensation unless the offender is identified and convicted.

A third alternative would be to allow victims who were uninsured and who had suffered hardship by the offence to claim against an expanded CICB scheme for personal injury below the present £400 limit and for small property losses. These are the victims who, in our view, do most obviously deserve government assistance. It reflects a preference articulated by the Court of Appeal when offenders in a single case had insufficient means to compensate all their victims. Rather than give each a *pro rata* share, the Court thought it preferable to give the individual victims their full loss and leave the one institutional sufferer (a bank) to bring a civil action.[57] We have not been able to ascertain for ourselves how much such a scheme would cost. The only way to gauge this, and the extra administrative problems it would create, would be to experiment with a pilot scheme. This we strongly recommend.[58]

Some of our committee are concerned that even this limited scheme would supplant the proper role of insurance companies. The majority do not share this view. The victims for whom we are

---

57. *R v. Amey and James*. (above, note 53).
58. Martin Iredale on practical grounds disassociates himself from this recommendation which he considers unrealistic.

concerned often live in areas of our cities where insurance of this kind is either unobtainable or can only be bought on payment of prohibitively expensive premiums.

(8) Compensation without prosecution

Compensation orders are not confined to offences of which offenders have been convicted. They can be made in juvenile courts, where offenders are 'found guilty', not convicted. They can also be used to ensure compensation for offences that, at the offender's request, the court agrees to 'take into consideration' when sentencing him.

(a) Offences taken into consideration[59]

The practice of 'taking offences into consideration' is very convenient since it allows the defendant to wipe the slate clean (or perhaps in some cases, almost clean) and increases the number of offences that are cleared up. The status of an offence taken into consideration is, though, unclear. It does not rank as a conviction and so cannot be the basis of a defence of *autrefois convict*.[60] On the other hand, it is treated in court as very similar to a guilty plea. Thus, each offence must be put to the defendant who must personally (and not through counsel) say whether he or she wishes that offence to be taken into consideration.[61]

The Powers of Criminal Courts Act 1973 is unusual in giving express recognition to this practice which has been built up entirely on the courts' initiative. The Act allows a court to order compensation for offences taken into consideration.[62] We approve of this, but there can be procedural difficulties which need attention.

Firstly, it is essential that the police or prosecution investigate information about possible loss caused by the offence before agreeing to allow it to be taken into consideration and our recommendation that the court be required to consider compensation is particularly important in the case of offences taken into consideration.

A second problem relates to the limited powers of magistrates who can only order up to £1000 compensation for each charge on which the defendant is convicted. The ceiling is not raised further if other offences are taken into consideration.[63] Thus, if a defendant is convicted of two charges and asks for ten more to be taken into consideration, the compensation for all twelve charges could not exceed

59. See Prof. H.A. Street, 'Offences Taken Into Consideration: Compensation Orders and the Trade Descriptions Act 1981' [1974] Crim. L.R. 345.
60. *R v. Nicholson* [1947] 2 All ER 535.
61. *DPP v. Anderson* [1978] A.C. 964.
62. 1973 Act sect. 35(1).
63. *Ibid.*, sect. 35(5).

£2000. This ceiling is academic in the case of most defendants whose means would anyway limit the amount that could be ordered, but it is a very real problem where the defendant is a person of substance or a business with adequate assets. It has been noted, for instance, by Professor Street in connection with offences by travel agents under the Trade Descriptions Act 1968[64] whose brochures may have mis-described thousands of holidays. Many customers may have suffered spoilt vacations as a result. Of course, the inadequacy of the Court's powers to deal with the totality of the offences would be a good reason for *not* dealing with the publication by way of a 'sample charge' and taking the additional matters into consideration.[65] If the other matters were the subject of other charges in another district, their prosecutor ought to be able to object to the charges being dealt with compendiously and should be given notice that this is being proposed. However it may be that the authorities would be happy to avoid the cost of further prosecutions and would not object. If the disappointed consumers were unwilling to take over the prosecution privately this would effectively preclude them from obtaining full compensation through the criminal courts. This is a regrettable but inevitable consequence of channelling prosecutions through a government official. If complainants have no right to insist that such a prosecution be initiated, we can see no basis for giving them a veto over its abandonment.

(b) Cautioning

We considered whether there should be an extension of the power to order compensation to offences for which the offenders have been cautioned by the police in lieu of prosecution. This is now a frequent occurrence. In some police areas more than 50% of detected juvenile offenders who had committed indictable offences and more than 10% of detected adult indictable offenders are disposed of in this way, although in other police forces the practice is less common. Over all, the numbers are substantial, as Table 1 shows.

Not all of these offences are of a kind which are likely to justify a claim for compensation. Even young children, however, can do costly damage; and the 66,700 cases of theft by children or young persons must have included many cases in which the loss to the owner was not trivial. The adults' indictable offences alone number more than 14,500.

Clearly the problem of compensation in such cases cannot be dis-

---

64. See note 59 note.
65. The prosecution ought to withhold its consent only for a good reason. *R v. MacLean* [1911] 1 KB 332.

Table 1   Offenders cautioned by police, 1982

	Age-groups			
	10–13	*14–16*	*17–20*	*21 or older*
Indictable Offences				
Personal violence	1 100	2 300	400	1 300
Sexual offences	300	1 100	900	500
Burglary	6 000	5 000	200	100
Robbery	100	—	—	—
Theft and handling	34 300	32 400	2 000	8 400
Fraud and forgery	400	600	100	400
Criminal damage	1 100	800	100	100
Summary non-motoring offences	6 100	12 800	6 900	19 100

Source: Table 54 of the *Criminal Statistics, England and Wales 1982* which rounds figures to the nearest 100.

missed as insignificant, and its significance will increase as cautions become more common. This seems to us a desirable development; but it would be all the more acceptable if a decision to caution offenders instead of prosecuting them did not have the automatic consequence – as it does at the moment – of depriving their victims of the chance of compensation from a criminal court.

The Royal Commission on Criminal Procedure recommended that the procedure for cautioning offenders in lieu of prosecution should be made the subject of statute. This recommendation has not yet been implemented; but in February 1983 the Attorney General issued to all police forces the Director of Public Prosecution's 'Criteria for Prosecution', which lists a large number of considerations that are relevant to the decision whether to caution an offender. Most of them relate to the nature of the offence or the age and other characteristics of the offender. The document also indicates, however, that the attitude of the complainant is sometimes relevant; and in most police forces it has for some considerable time been the practice to consult the complainant before deciding to substitute a caution for prosecution. In some forces the instructions draw attention to the fact that if there is no prosecution the complainant cannot expect a compensation or restitution order. On the other hand, we were assured that the police would not offer a caution to an offender as an inducement to pay compensation.

The awkwardness of this situation lies in the fact that while some offenders may offer compensation (or restitution) in the hope that this will favourably affect the decision whether to prosecute or caution them, those who are fairly sure of being cautioned – for example because they fall into what is known to be a special category – have no great incentive to do so. Even those who have promised to do so cannot be compelled to keep their promises. The practice is that once a caution has been administered the offender is never subsequently prosecuted for the same offence; so that a caution is final, unlike, for instance, a conditional discharge.

We considered whether the practice could be improved without legislation. Clearly complainants who have suffered loss, damage or physical injury from an identified offender should be informed by the police of their right to ask a criminal court (or the Criminal Injuries Compensation Board, as the case may be) for compensation (or restitution). It would also be possible for the police to delay the decision to prosecute or caution until assured that the offender has in fact taken steps to compensate the complainant. Since the sums involved would not usually be large, this should not normally involve a long delay. Some of us feel, however, that this would involve the police to an undesirable extent in assessing the justice of victims' claims and the ability of defendants to pay, and we realise that to delay some cautions for this reason would be regarded as complicating the task of the police. It seems to us preferable, and in accordance with the recommendation of the Royal Commission on Criminal Procedure, to propose a solution which would involve legislation. It would not be the first piece of legislation to take statutory notice of the practice of cautioning: sect. 2 of the Street Offences Act 1959 already does so in the cases of cautions for soliciting. What we have in mind is that it should be made possible for evidence of a caution to be produced to a magistrates' court by a complainant who has a 'clear case' for compensation or restitution. With this in view, an offender who is cautioned should sign an admission of his offence and a copy should be given to the victim. Since cautions are administered only when offenders admit their guilt, this should present no problem; and it seems a desirable procedure even when a claim is unlikely. The Court would not be obliged to grant a compensation or restitution order automatically. It might consider for example that there was no 'clear case', in which event the complainant's only present recourse would be to bring a civil suit, but the offender's signed admission ought to be admissible in a civil court (as evidence of a conviction is at present). Compensation or restitution orders made by a magistrates' court in such cases should be enforceable in the same ways as those made after a conviction (or a finding of guilt in a juvenile court).[66]

66. We realise that in some cases enforcement might lead to imprisonment (although that is an infrequent result of compensation orders). These would not, however, be the only circumstances in which an unconvicted offender could be imprisoned for defaulting a payment: it can happen in the case unpaid recognisances by sureties or after a bind over – see also Criminal Justice Act 1982 Sched. 4.

This proposal seems to us to have more than one attraction. It interferes as little as possible with the policy and procedure for cautioning offenders. At the same time, it would mean that a caution no longer debarred victims with modest claims for compensation or restitution from seeking the necessary order in a magistrates' court instead of the civil courts, with their attendant complications and delays. It would thus remove one obstacle to what we regard as a desirable development, the increased use of cautions in lieu of prosecutions in cases in which this is otherwise in the public interest.

(9) Sample charges

There is one further matter which needs to be considered both in connection with compensation and confiscation and is we think better considered under the latter heading (see chapter 6). At present a compensation order can only be made in respect of an offence of which the offender has either been found guilty or one which he has asked to be taken into consideration. Is this limitation necessary and just? Take the case of an employee who systematically defrauds his employer by making excessive requisitions for expenses. Eventually the discrepancy between his expenses and those of others in comparable employment is noted and watch is kept and evidence gathered which justifies the bringing of charges relating to specific periods. If it is clear from a comparison between these periods and those where no watch was kept that exactly the same fraud was being committed in the unwatched periods, should not there be some way in which the employer could be compensated for what he has lost in total? It is a much less satisfactory way of achieving redress for the Court itself roughly to assess the amount of profit and impose a fine of that amount.

6   Confiscation

This Committee was set up in part because of concern over the 'Operation Julie' case; it follows that the question of confiscating the proceeds of crime has been one of our major concerns. When there is no identifiable victim who can be compensated the criminal law provides no direct means of confiscating the proceeds of crime as such although sometimes a fine can be so calculated as to achieve the same result. Offences that involve no immediate victim and no civil liability resulting from their commission can however cause massive social harm; we call them in this report 'non-victim offences'.

In our discussion paper we asked the simple sounding question: 'Should the courts be given a new power to confiscate the proceeds of crime?' Among ourselves and all whom we have consulted that question was answered 'yes'. It was when we came to consider what limits, if any, should be set and, even more difficult, how any new power could be enforced that we became aware of the problems involved.

We have seen in chapter 5 how by legislative provision and judicial decision limits have been set upon the criminal courts' power to award compensation to the victim of crime. Of these the 'clear case' limitation has been set by the judges on grounds of expediency. It is felt that the present unsatisfactory delays in the bringing to trial of criminal cases would be further exacerbated if difficult cases of compensation fell to be decided by the criminal courts. This limitation on the powers of criminal courts to award compensation is acceptable only because victims have their civil remedies and their right to apply for compensation to the Criminal Injuries Compensation Board where they have suffered personal injury. Obviously, no power to confiscate the profits of crime could be so limited: it would be intolerable to restrict the power of confiscation to clear cases. New procedures must be sufficiently sophisticated to deal with complex cases.

We consider (in chapter 9) the question of what pre-trial restraint will be essential if effective use is to be made of any new powers of confiscation and more effective use of the criminal courts' powers to make compensation orders. We consider in this chapter what procedures can be devised after conviction to effect confiscation. We have found that equally difficult problems arise.

Categories of profitable non-victim offences

At an early stage we identified three broad categories of non-victim offending. First, there are those serious offences where it would be unacceptable to rely solely upon confiscating the proceeds as redress for the offending and where penal sanctions are called for in addition. Serious drug offences such as were revealed by Operation Julie itself and corruption in public office exemplify this category.

Second, there are those offences that involve serious dishonesty or extensive trading in prohibited goods, but which it is or may become acceptable to meet with redress by confiscation of the gains together with, in some cases perhaps, a further monetary penalty.

Our third category of non-victim offences covers those contraventions of regulations that involve little or no public obloquy but where the profits made from the offence far outweigh, in many cases, any penalty exacted.[1] The demolition of a listed building, the felling of protected trees, the systematic overloading of vehicles and the pollution of the environment are some of the ways in which hugh profits are made from breaking the law.

Most offences of fraud and dishonesty have as their victims individuals whose identity is known or ascertainable; redress in these cases belongs in the sphere of compensation. However, there are two categories of fraudulent offending where the state itself is the victim, namely revenue and excise frauds; the way in which most such offences are dealt with is a curious feature of our criminal justice system. In the great majority of cases such frauds are dealt with by the exaction of a penalty without any criminal prosecution.

The powers given to the Commissioners of Inland Revenue ('the Board') and the Commissioners of Customs and Excise ('the Commissioners') are extraordinarily wide. Those of the Board are set out in sect. 102 of the Taxes Management Act 1970.

The Board may in their discretion mitigate any penalty, or stay or compound any proceedings for recovery thereof, and may also, after judgment, further mitigate or entirely remit the penalty.

Those of the Commissioners are specified in sect. 152 of the Customs and Excise Management Act 1979.

The Commissioners may, as they see fit,

(a) stay, sist or compound any proceedings for an offence or for the condemnation of anything as being forfeited under the customs and excise Acts; or
(b) restore, subject to such conditions (if any) as they think proper, any thing forfeited or seized under those Acts; or

1. See for instance *St. John Shipping Corp v. Joseph Rank Ltd* [1957] QB 267.

(c) after judgment, mitigate or remit any pecuniary penalty imposed under those Acts; or

(d) order any person who has been imprisoned to be discharged before the expiration of his term of imprisonment being a person imprisoned for any offence under those Acts or in respect of the non-payment of a penalty or other sum adjudged to be paid or awarded in relation to such an offence or in respect of the default of a sufficient distress to satisfy such a sum;

but paragraph (a) above shall not apply to proceedings on indictment in Scotland.

The power of the Commissioners to order, by executive action, the discharge of a prisoner is, we believe, unique in our law and rarely used.[2] However, the extent to which the other powers are used is very considerable. In some 90% of VAT fraud cases the Commissioners offer to compound a penalty,[3] that is to agree not to prosecute a person against whom they believe they have sufficient evidence in exchange for payment of the tax due together with a variable penalty.[4] The use of compounding by the Commissioners has grown dramatically since the 1950s, when it was virtually confined to passenger baggage offences.[5] The Commissioners sometimes consider compounding when the unpaid tax is very large indeed. In 1981, in an operation called 'Nudger', a VAT fraud involving £2,700,000 was compounded and criminal proceedings stayed.[6]

Compounding offences by the Board is also widespread. It is quite normal for compounding to take place after a taxpayer has sworn a statement as to his true earnings or profits and, other than in very serious cases, only if a sworn statement proves to be incorrect is there a prosecution. To a limited extent settlements are negotiable and the penalty above the payment of the actual tax outstanding, although often substantial, is rarely the maximum which could have been levied.

This way of treating people who have offended against the criminal

2. The only occasion in the last thirty years concerned Glenstone Page Laws, whose sentence of nine years for smuggling heroin into the US was reduced to allow his immediate release and thereby his return to the US (his country of nationality) where he was both a defendant and a prosecution witness in an American drug smuggling trial. House of Commons written answer by John Moore 7 November 1983.

3. *Keith Report on Enforcement Powers of Revenue Departments*, Cmnd 8822, (1983), para 16.4.3.

4. The Commissioners of Customs and Excise have the power to compound offences under the VAT Code or Customs and Excise legislation. Customs and Excise Management Act 1979 sect. 152(1), Finance Act 1972 sect. 38(8). Similarly the Board of Inland Revenue can mitigate penalties or compound proceedings. Taxes Management Act 1970 sect. 102.

5. Keith Report, para 16.4.3.

6. Keith Report, note 35.

law has attracted judicial praise for its efficiency, and cost effectiveness,[7] but the fact that offenders, in most cases, remain anonymous
has attracted criticism. In 1983 the Keith Committee on the Enforcement Powers of Revenue Departments recommended that although
the tax authorities should be able to compound or make settlements,
the names of the persons concerned should be publicised, except
where there had been full spontaneous voluntary disclosure.[8]

The way in which revenue offences are dealt with without recourse
to the courts suggest that similar advantages might be obtained if the
same sort of administrative action were possible in the case of a wider
range of other offences. But, in any event, it certainly suggests that
there would be nothing wrong in principle or unacceptable in practice
if redress by the courts begins to take precedence over punishment in
cases of non-victim offending. Revenue offences are often of substantially greater criminality than those regularly prosecuted in the
criminal courts.

(1) The scope of a new confiscation power

We have seen in chapter 4 how most countries with a civil law (as
opposed to common law) system have provisions simply allowing or
requiring a court to confiscate the product or profit of an offence, and
we think that there would be no insuperable difficulty in giving
similar general powers to the criminal courts in this country. But for a
number of different reasons we have come to the conclusion that a
provision of general application to all offences would be not only
impracticable but, in some cases, also arguably unjust. It would be
impracticable because the new procedures which will be necessary for
enforcement would not be justified in cases of minor contraventions;
it would perhaps be unjust because in some cases, such as soliciting
for prostitution, it might add substantially and unacceptably to the
penalty for the offence.

We considered whether it would be possible to list those offences
where the remedy of confiscation should be made available but we
think that that would be wholly impracticable.[9] Another possibility is
that confiscation should be limited to 'serious crime', defined perhaps
as offences carrying the possible sanction of a prison sentence, but this
would exclude many of the profitable regulatory offences which we
think should clearly be included.

7. For example, *Patel v. Spence* [1976] 1 WLR 1268, 1270 *A-G v. Johnstone* (1926) 10
   T.C. 758.
8. Keith Report, paras 18.5.54 and 20.2.11–12.
9. See a report by Justice, 'Breaking the Rules. The Problem of Crimes and Contraventions', where the impracticability of any such categorisation, in a different
   context, is considered.

In the end we have concluded that a limit related, though not perhaps directly, to the amount of money involved should be set. The fine is a blunt instrument which can be used to take back from offenders any profit which they have made. In many cases where the amount of profit made is clear this blunt instrument is also effective and just. This will be so in many cases in the magistrates' court and we are of the opinion therefore that the power of confiscation should be given only to the crown court.

We appreciate that this will involve amending the law to permit magistrates to commit cases to the crown court for consideration of confiscation where, at present, the offence is triable only summarily. So long as the committal is for confiscation purposes only we see no objection to this.

We have considered whether any upper financial limit should be set to the power of the crown court to make a confiscation order. We think not. Whether confiscation orders are made and appropriate confiscation procedures ordered in any particular case can be safely left to the discretion of the crown court judge. We think, however, that in exactly the same way as we believe courts should be required to consider whether a compensation order should be made (see chapter 5), so the crown court should be required to consider whether a confiscation order should be made or confiscation procedures invoked in all cases where it seems that substantial profit may have been made from offending, and magistrates' courts should similarly be required to consider in such cases whether to commit to the crown court for consideration of confiscation.

In the same way as issues of compensation range from the simple to the complex so will issues of confiscation. As far as possible we think that confiscation orders should be made immediately upon conviction. This will require new rules of procedure. We think that, in those cases where the prosecution takes place in the crown court, the prosecuting authority should serve on the defendant notice that it will, if the defendant is convicted, ask for a confiscation order, where it believes the profit can be easily calculated, or, where calculation is more complex, that it will ask for an enquiry into the profits. In cases that have come from the magistrates' court the prosecution should, in the same way, particularise its claim.

(2) Objective of confiscation

We have considered what should be the objective of a confiscation order. We think it should be to restore the *status quo* before the offence. This would require confiscation of only the net profits of offending (see the analogous civil procedures considered in chapter 3).

If drug traffickers have paid their suppliers, confiscation of the gross proceeds would go further than would be necessary to put them in the same position as if they had not offended. Similarly, the owner of a listed building will no doubt have had to incur expense in demolishing it; the Court need only confiscate the amount by which the value of the land has been increased less these expenses to ensure that no profit is made from the offence. Of course, some additional penalty may be appropriate, but this ought to be considered separately and openly and not imposed under the guise of confiscation.

(3) Burden of proof

The burden of proof should, we think, be allocated differently on the basis of income and expenditure. The Crown ought to prove the amount of gross proceeds. Where it is impossible to trace the actual receipts from the sale of an illegal commodity it must be made clear that evidence of the police or enforcement agencies, such as the Customs and Excise, as to their knowledge of prices should be admissible. For example, the 'street value' of a particular quantity of a prohibited drug would be proveable in this way. This would raise a rebuttable presumption that the defendant had received these amounts. The burden would then be on the defendant to show that he has been paid less and to show any expenses that reduced the net profit he had made. The expenses ought only to be allowable if actually paid; any uncompleted promise to pay his suppliers may well be unenforceable as illegal contracts (chapter 3). Consideration could also be given to making the deduction of expenses contingent on disclosure of the identity of the payee. If an offender preferred to suffer a heavier penalty than to 'grass' on others that is not a matter of concern to us.

We believe that, not infrequently, the prosecution and defence will be able openly to compromise at an agreed figure. Such an agreement would only be reached after conviction or on a plea of guilty and, subject to what we say in chapter 14, we can see no objection to this. We consider what should be done when the trial judge cannot himself decide on the amount to confiscate after we have looked at the question whether a confiscation order should be available to the courts in respect of offences other than those charged and proved or specifically admitted.

(4) Sample counts

In relation to both compensation orders and confiscation orders questions are raised by the now accepted practice of charging sample counts where a course of conduct has consisted in a large number of small offences. The practice of charging only enough specimen charges to indicate a system is actively encouraged by the courts, but where redress either by compensating the victim or victims or by confiscating the profits of crime is concerned, it causes difficulties which have been of much concern to us. The speedy and efficient disposal of criminal cases demands that indictments shall be kept as short and simple as possible. But where only specimen counts are before a jury a verdict is only possible on those counts, and unless the defendant is prepared to admit the whole of the defalcations and ask for them to be taken into consideration they cannot found a compensation or restitution order or to be taken into account in deciding whether the relevant offences for the purpose of making a criminal bankruptcy order exceed £15,000.

In *DPP v. Anderson*[10] a man was convicted on thirteen counts of offences of obtaining money by deception from his employers to the value of £7112. A schedule to the indictment set out twenty alleged similar offences involving some £19,600. The thirteen counts on which he was convicted were stated to be 'sample counts', but at the end of the trial the defendant did not agree to the twenty further alleged offences being taken into consideration. The trial judge nevertheless made a criminal bankruptcy order on the basis of both sets of alleged offences; on the thirteen convictions he could not have done so because they did not exceed £15,000. The House of Lords said he was wrong in doing this and quashed the bankruptcy order.

Lord Wilberforce showed concern at the restrictive nature of the criminal bankruptcy legislation. He said of it

'Unfortunately, this beneficial legislation has been conferred in restrictive terms; in this it follows the pattern set by the Theft Act 1968 sect. 28 (which deals with restitution) and in the sections dealing with compensation orders (sects. 35 to 38 of the 1973 Act). In this respect English law has always lagged behind other systems in enabling persons suffering loss as the result of criminal conduct to recover their property, or compensation for the loss of it, in one set of proceedings rather than in two.

And he concluded his speech;

If the criminal bankruptcy procedure is to be workable, without the necessity to multiply charges, it would seem that either the sum of £15,000 should be changed, or that a wider discretion as to the existence, or apparent existence, of other losses than those involved in the offences on which the person concerned was convicted, must be given to the trial judge.[11]

Both Lord Diplock and Lord Salmon expressed approval of the

---

10. [1978] 2 All ER 512.
11. *Ibid.*, pp. 513–14.

system of charging sample counts but Lord Diplock did not echo Lord Wilberforce's concern at the restrictive nature of the legislation concerning criminal bankruptcy, restitution and compensation. He said 'if justice is to be done it is essential that the practice [of taking uncharged offences into consideration] should not be followed except with the express and unequivocal consent of the offender himself'. The last paragraph of his speech should perhaps be cited in full.

Nothing that I have said should be understood as discouraging the practice of limiting the charges in an indictment to a limited number of 'sample' counts in cases where, as in the instance case, the accused has adopted a systematic dishonest practice. Your Lordships were told that, where sample counts are used, it is customary to provide the defence with a list of all the similar offences of which it alleged that those selected as the subject of the counts contained in the indictment are samples. In appropriate cases it may be that evidence of all or some of these additional offences is led by the prosecution at the trial as evidence of 'system', as was apparently done in the instant case. In other cases, the additional offences in the schedule are not referred to until after a verdict of guilty has been returned. The judge is then told of the total amount involved in the systematic offences of which those charged in the indictment have been selected by the prosecution as samples. Where sample counts are used it is, in my view, essential that the ordinary procedure should be followed for taking other offences into consideration in determining sentence. The accused should be given an opportunity after the verdict to consider the schedule of other offences which he is alleged by the prosecution to have committed and should be explicitly asked by the judge which of them he admits and whether he wishes them to be taken into consideration. Only if he agrees to that course may such offences be included in calculating the amount for which a criminal bankruptcy order may be made under sect. 39 of the Act or a compensation order under sect. 35.[12]

Anderson's case was concerned only with a criminal bankruptcy order. Paradoxically, although where criminal bankruptcy, compensation and restitution are concerned the courts' powers are limited by the wording of the various enactments, where other sentences are concerned, the judge is, it seems, entitled to act on the basis of the whole course of conduct whether charged or not. In *R v. Price*[13] the Court of Appeal, presided over by the present Lord Chief Justice, specifically found that the trial judge had adopted the right basis for sentencing in relation to the 'reality of the situation', which was that the appellant had committed an ascertainable number of offences which were represented by the single specimen offence considered by the jury. The Court distinguished *Anderson* on the ground that, in *Anderson*, the House of Lords was 'considering, and considering

12. *Ibid.*, p. 516.
13. [1979] Crim. L. R. 468.

simply, the provisions of sect. 39 of the Powers of Criminal Courts Act 1973'. The Court of Appeal in *R v. Singh*[14] reached the same conclusion.

On the basis of these authorities it is possible to state what seems to be the present legal position where sample counts are charged. In doing so we use the phrase 'redress order' as a comprehensive description of compensation, restitution and criminal bankruptcy orders and contrast it with 'penalties' such as imprisonment, community service orders and fines. We must also stress that we are here concerned only with cases where sample counts are charged. Where there is evidence produced at trial that tends to show that a defendant is guilty of offences other than those charged, not being the background offences of which those actually charged are samples, there can be no doubt that the judge should not take those alleged offences into account in sentencing the defendant.[15]

The legal position seems to be that where sample counts are charged, the sentencer may impose a penalty on the basis of the whole history of the matter as disclosed by the evidence or, as it was put in *Price*, 'in relation to the reality of the situation'. However he can only make a redress order on the basis of those offences of which the defendant has actually been found guilty together with those offences which he has explicitly admitted and asked to have taken into consideration.

We are not primarily concerned with penalties but with redress, and the present state of the law is unsatisfactory. This can be plainly demonstrated by adding some hypotheses to the facts of *Anderson's* case. Let us assume for the purposes of demonstration these additional or different facts:

(1) that the defendant was guilty of the twenty offences;
(2) that he was possessed of money or property to a total value of, let us say, £60,000;
(3) that the judge felt that, in all the circumstances, he did not need to impose a custodial sentence, or at any rate, not an immediate custodial sentence; and
(4) that the judge wanted to achieve as great a redress of the wrong done as he could.

If those assumptions are made what can the judge do? He can make a compensation order but that would be limited to the £7112 represented by the thirteen offences of which the defendant was convicted.

14. (1981) 1 Crim App. R. (S)90.
15. *R v. Wishart* (1979) 1 Crim. App. R. (S) 322.

However, he can take into account the 'reality of the situation' in deciding what penalty to impose. He wishes to relieve the defendant of all his ill-gotten gains, but the only way he can do this is by imposing a fine. He decides that the fine should exceed the gains made so he fines in the amount of £25,000. The result of that sentence is that the defendant is mulcted in the sum of £32,000.

Now let us suppose that his employers decide to recover the additional £19,600 in a civil action. In that action they will only have to establish the defendant's indebtedness on a balance of probabilities not to the extent of certainty demanded by a criminal trial. Clearly therefore they will get judgment. What now is the position of the defendant? He has had to pay £51,000 and he is still, in theory though not in practice, at risk of further prosecution for the outstanding twenty offences. Such a result can, plainly, not be justified.

The imposition of penalties on the basis of offences which have neither been charged nor which the defendant has asked to have taken into consideration has been criticised.[16] But, if the only way in which the Crown can make sure that the Court will be able to make a redress order is by charging every single offence alleged to have been committed in a course of dealing, this will inevitably lead to what Lord Salmon in *Anderson* said would be a 'wholly unnecessary prolongation of trials resulting in a shocking waste of public time and money'. We believe[17] that, with more stringent safeguards and a more formal procedure than the *ad hoc* method described by Lord Diplock in *Anderson*, the judge should, in cases were the courts charged are specifically stated to be sample counts, be entitled to take into account the reality of the offending as disclosed by the evidence adduced. But any additional power should be subject to clearly defined statutory limitations.

In framing a new confiscation order and in considering whether and to what extent the ambit of the present redress orders ought to be enlarged, there are two main matters of concern: that crime should not pay and that no injustice should be done. To the extent that these two principles are incompatible the second should plainly prevail. The aim must therefore be to frame legislation which covers as wide an ambit of wrongdoing as possible without doing or seeming to do injustice to anyone.

First, we think it would be essential that the prosecution should formally give notice to the defence that the charges upon which it is proceeding are 'sample counts'. This is something which, in any

16. By D.A. Thomas; see for example [1979] Crim. L.R. 509.
17. This view is not shared by Andrew Nicol and Clive Soley. See their Note of Dissent page 144.

event, is now openly stated at trial. Second, the prosecution should serve notice on the defendant that, in the event of conviction on those counts, it will seek compensation or confiscation on the basis of illegal dealing. The period of alleged illegal dealing should be clearly stated and should be supported by the evidence disclosed in the depositions. If, for any reason, evidence of illegal dealing would be inadmissible in the trial it should be set out in the form of additional depositions in the notice. The defendant would then know that if he failed to combat successfully the actual charges brought against him he would face further investigation, the precise nature of which and the additional evidence, if any, to be adduced would be clear to him. It should be clearly stated in the legislation that service of such a notice would preclude future prosecution for any offences included in the notice.

We envisage the procedure at the end of a trial where there has been a conviction on sample counts to be of this nature. First, the defendant would be asked whether he admitted all or any of the matters contained in the prosecution notice. If he did not admit them, or any of them, he or his counsel would be asked to submit on what grounds the defendant's denial was based. It seems to us that there could, in practice, be but two reasons: one that the evidence adduced at the trial did not establish that the offences alleged in the notice had been committed, the other that the additional evidence included in the notice (if any) was challenged. If the first objection is raised we see no reason why the judge should not hear argument and give a decision, with reasons, before making a redress order. In the second the disputed evidence could be called and again the judge could decide on its credibility. It must be remembered that, at this stage, there is no question of criminal liability; all the judge is deciding is whether in respect of the additional matters a claim for compensation, restitution or confiscation has been established. In cases of redress only, therefore, there seems no reason why the judge should apply any burden of proof other than the balance of probabilities. However, if doubts persist as to the justice of the present system of imposing penalties it may be that some such procedure as we have suggested could be required before any sentence was passed which took account of the scheduled offences; in that case the burden should be that necessary to establish criminal liability.

We believe that so long as the counts charged are genuine sample counts, were this procedure or something like it to be provided, the defendant would, in the vast majority of cases, when found guilty on the sample counts admit the scheduled counts as well.

When there are sample counts we believe that, as with straightforward cases, the trial judge should, whenever possible, himself make the confiscation order at the time of sentence. However there will undoubtedly arise from time to time cases (whether straight-forward or sample cases) of such complexity that a separate enquiry will have to be undertaken by someone. We do not underestimate the complexities which would arise in fashioning legislation to meet these comparatively rare cases. Each case will require detailed investigation and new procedures will have to be provided. What is needed is some procedure of an investigative nature such as it was hoped could be provided by a criminal bankruptcy order in cases where compensation issues arise. We envisage a procedure whereby the judge makes an order for an enquiry into profit; the proceedings would be analogous to the civil procedures for directing an account to be taken (see chapter 3). Pre-trial restraints, powers to trace assets and impose sequestration will be needed to make the sanction effective (see chapter 9).

(5) Confiscation and imprisonment

Orders for an enquiry should only be made where the profits are clearly substantial, but where such an enquiry has to be ordered something will have to be done to defer or partially defer sentence. In cases where, in any event, the defendants are not going to be deprived of their liberty we see no problem in this. Sentence will be deferred pending a report on the enquiry being made to the Court. The Court will then be in a position to make a confiscation order and, if thought fit, impose a further monetary penalty. In coming to that sentencing decision we see no reason why the Court should not be empowered to take into account any comments as to the co-operation or lack of co-operation of the offender in the enquiry. But in no case should a sentence of imprisonment be imposed. This would be in line with current practice on deferred sentences (see chapter 14).

Nor do we see any particular difficulty in a case where the Court has decided that although a sentence of imprisonment is necessary, it can, in any event, be wholly suspended. In such cases the sentence of imprisonment could be passed at once and suspended and imposition of further monetary penalty by way of confiscation and/or fine deferred pending enquiry as to profit. Of course, no report to the Court therefore, however critical of the defendant's lack of co-operation, could justify activation of the suspended sentence.

Difficulty arises where an immediate deprivation of liberty has to be imposed. That decision must of course be made irrespective of any question of confiscation and should, in our view, be made immedi-ately upon conviction, again in line with present policy in deciding whether to defer sentence. In cases where confiscation issues have been either decided by evidence at trial or compromise at the time of sentencing we see no reason, subject to what we say in chapter 14, why that should not be taken into account in fixing the period of imprisonment. Where an immediate sentence of imprisonment is imposed, but confiscation issues have to be made the subject of an enquiry, we see no reason why the Court should not, if the report on the enquiry is favourable to the defendant and indicates that he has co-operated fully, take that into account and, in its light, reduce the period of imprisonment. Of course, in no case should a sentence of imprisonment be capable of being increased as a result of an unfavourable report. But to take into account, retrospectively, co-operation in a redress investigation seems as unobjectionable to us as to take into account, in mitigation of penalty, a plea of guilty.

Reversed burden of proof

As a general rule no member of the Committee would go further than this. However we have seen in chapter 4 that in some jurisdictions when particular concern is felt as to the profits earned in certain forms of offending, more draconian measures have been introduced. In the United States and Australia illegal drug trafficking (and in the United States, racketeering) are examples; in Hong Kong corruption offences are similarly treated. The customs law in Australia allows the courts to assess a pecuniary penalty to represent the proceeds of illegal drug trafficking. A specific conviction is not an essential pre-condition of the penalty. Futhermore, the proceeds can be calculated *prima facie* as the increase in value of the defendant's assets between the first offence and the last. The burden is then on the defendant to show that he came by the increase lawfully. Similar presumptions and reversals of the burden of proof are contained in the Hong Kong Anti-Corruption Ordinance.

As we have said, we would not recommend any general rules of this sort. Nor do we think that corruption and racketeering are so prevalent in and disruptive of our society as to merit special treatment. Whether such procedures would be justified in the case of wholesale trafficking in drugs is a matter upon which our Committee is divided. The majority believe that anyone convicted of wholesale trafficking in drugs should be liable to face more stringent investigation than would be appropriate for other forms of offending. The reasons advanced are that the trafficking in hard drugs inflicts such terrible social harm and is, by its nature, so difficult to detect, that when a wholesaler is caught and convicted condign measures are justified to ensure that he enters prison stripped of all his ill-gotten gains. We are not here speaking of mere couriers or retailers but of their employers, and we believe that any new investigative procedures should be limited to those convicted of supplying hard drugs in substantial amounts. The requirement should be conviction of supplying Class A or B drugs to a street value of perhaps as much as £100,000. On such a conviction the majority of the Committee believes that the judge should be entitled to order a wide-ranging investigation into the defendant's finances. The prosecution seeking such an order should be required to state and prove the date at which a first offence took place and any investigation should be limited to the period subsequent to that date. In any such investigation there should be no objection to the imposition of similar burdens on the offender as those imposed in the Australian and Hong Kong legislation or the tracing of profits made illegally into the hands of family and friends. The defendant should have relief from prosecution in relation to any offence disclosed by him in the investigation.

In cases of wholesale drug trafficking the Court itself will rarely be able to estimate the amount of profit; nor will there often be any agreement, we think, between prosecution and defence. By definition, the defendant will be facing a long prison sentence. However what we said previously about co-operation should, we think, apply equally to these offenders.

Other members of the Committee[18] would oppose these measures even for those convicted of supplying large amounts of listed drugs. In their view, our principles of criminal procedure are tested most strongly where defendants are unpopular or have been accused of the most offensive behaviour but they ought to withstand that test. One of the most basic principles is that a person is presumed innocent until proved guilty. This now forms part of the European Convention on Human Rights (Article 6(2)). That presumption must mean that a defendant is entitled to stay silent, to be unco-operative, to insist that the Crown prove its case without his or her help.

The view expressed by the other members of the Committee conflicts with this principle. It is true that they would cast the burden of explaining the cause of their wealth on defendants only after they have been convicted of *an* offence. In this respect their proposal is an improvement on the Australian law where confiscation procedures may be initiated without any criminal conviction. However, so far as defendants have been convicted of identified offences, there is no need for the enquiry which the other members propose. In respect of these offences the Court might in the future invoke the powers of confiscation which were recommended earlier in the chapter. Rather, the purpose of the enquiry and the object of placing on the defendant the

18. Andrew Nicol, Clive Soley and Anthony Leifer.

duty to explain the origin of his or her assets would be to uncover further suspected offences. In this, the proposal clashes directly with the presumption of innocence. If defendants stay silent they may be penalised by having their assets confiscated, though the Crown has not linked their property to the offences of which they were convicted, and though the Crown has introduced no evidence of their complicity in other offences. In the view of these members the presumption of innocence should apply to each separate allegation of criminality and not be overturned by the defendant's conviction of other, distinct offences. In this respect Andrew Nicol and Clive Soley believe that the recommendation shares the vice of the proposal made by the other committee members for dealing with sample counts. These objections are elaborated in a Note of Dissent but in short that proposal, like the current one, undermines the normal and proper method for determining a person's complicity in a serious criminal offence. Anthony Leifer believes that while the sample count procedure may be justified, the reversal of the burden of proof is a greater and more significant intrusion on a defendant's rights and is not justifiable.

7 Restitution

The principal[1] power enabling a criminal court to order property to be restored to its rightful owner is contained in sect. 28 of the Theft Act 1968.

28. (1) Where goods have been stolen, and either a person is convicted of any offence with reference to the theft (whether or not the stealing is the gist of his offence) or a person is convicted of any other offence but such an offence as aforesaid is taken into consideration in determining his sentence, the court by or before which the offender is convicted may on the conviction (whether or not the passing of sentence is in other respects deferred) exercise any of the following powers –

(a) the court may order anyone having possession or control of the goods to restore them to any person entitled to recover them from him; or

(b) on the application of a person entitled to recover from the person convicted any other goods directly or indirectly representing the first-mentioned goods (as being the proceeds of any disposal or realisation of the whole or part of them or of goods so representing them), the court may order those other goods to be delivered or transferred to the applicant; or

(c) the court may order that a sum not exceeding the value of the first-mentioned goods shall be paid, out of any money of the person convicted which was taken out of his possession on his apprehension, to any person who, if those goods were in the possession of the person convicted, would be entitled to recover them from him.

(2) Where under subsection (1) above the court has power on a person's conviction to make an order against him both under paragraph (b) and under paragraph (c) with reference to the stealing of the same goods, the court may make orders under both paragraphs provided that the person in whose favour the orders are made does not thereby recover more than the value of those goods.

(3) Where under subsection (1) above the court on a person's conviction makes an order under paragraph (a) for the restoration of any goods, and it appears to the court that the person convicted has sold the goods to a person acting in good faith, or has borrowed money on the security of them from a person so acting, the court may order that there shall be paid to the purchaser or lender, out of any money of the person convicted which was taken out of his possession on his apprehension, a sum not exceeding the amount paid for the

---

1. Magistrates also have a power to order delivery of property in the hands of the police to 'the person appearing . . . to be the owner thereof'. Police (Property) Act 1897 sect. 1(1).

purchase by the purchaser or, as the case may be, the amount owed to the lender in respect of the loan.

(4) The court shall not exercise the powers conferred by this section unless in the opinion of the court the relevant facts sufficiently appear from evidence given at the trial or the available documents, together with admissions made by or on behalf of any person in connection with any proposed exercise of the powers; and for this purpose 'the available documents' means any written statements or admissions which were made for use, and would have been admissible, as evidence at the trial, the depositions taken at any committal proceedings and any written statements or admissions used as evidence in those proceedings.

(5) Any order under this section shall be treated as an order for the restitution of property within the meaning of sects. 30 and 42 of the Criminal Appeal Act 1968 (which relate to the effect on such orders of appeals).

(6) References in this section to stealing are to be construed in accordance with sect. 24(1) and (4) of this Act.

Thus the courts may make three types of restitution orders. They may refer to

(1) the goods themselves if in the possession of the defendant: sect. 28 (1) (a)

(2) the goods themselves if in the possession of a third party (in this case the third party may be awarded compensation out of the money taken from the defendant at the time of his arrest) sect. 28(1) (d) and sect. 28(3)

(3) the proceeds of the goods or other property into which they have been converted. sect. 28(1)(b).

In each case the defendant must have been convicted of stealing the goods, obtaining them by deception, obtaining them by blackmail, or handling them.[2] Alternatively, a restitution order can be made if the defendant asks for one of these offences relating to the goods to be taken into consideration.[3]

(1)   The clear case requirement

We have seen that the courts have placed an important restriction on the power to order compensation, namely that the Court should only make an award in a 'clear case' (see chapter 5). There has been the same approach for the same reasons of expediency in the case of restitution orders.[4] Just as the criminal courts cannot spare the time to resolve complicated issues of liability and quantum so it is said they ought not to undertake the task of resolving difficult questions of title. This was the opinion of the Criminal Law Revision Committee's

2. Theft Act 1968, sect. 24(1) and (4) and sect. 28(6).
3. *Ibid.*, sect. 28(1).
4. *R v. Ferguson* [1970] 2 All ER 820 C.A.

Report on which the Theft Act 1968 was based.[5] Our views on this are exactly the same as we have expressed in respect of the 'clear case' restriction in compensation (see p. 56). We are strongly of the opinion that the more frequently the criminal court can redress wrongs and help the victims of crime the better.

It may be that sect. 28(4) reflected the attitude of the courts in restricting cases where restitution orders are made to simple cases. What it says, and all that it says, is that you cannot make an order for restitution unless such an order is justified by the evidence already before the court in the criminal trial. It also may have some of its origins in an attitude, now becoming outmoded, that, after conviction, the prosecution has no further part to play in assisting the court.[6] But it is clear from the provision of the Criminal Justice Act 1982 relating to compensation[7] that the prosecution may present evidence and make representation after conviction with a view to persuading the court to make a compensation order (see chapter 5). We can see no reason why, in cases where there is a question whether a restitution order should be made, the prosecution should not play a full part in assisting the court by calling further evidence or by argument.

(2) Restitution subject to an allowance

Compensation orders made by criminal courts are in a way a method of short-circuiting civil proceedings. In chapter 5 we expressed the view that they should not be used where civil proceedings would not lead to the defendant being held liable.

We think that similar principles ought to be applied to restitution orders, and that they should not be used so as to leave the original owner better off than if the offence had not been committed. This could happen particularly in two contexts: first where the 'owner' has only a limited interest in the goods; second where the goods were improved after the owner lost them.

Some of the most important types of 'limited interests' are those of hire purchase companies. A hire purchase company usually buys goods from a retailer and then lets them out on hire to the customer. When a prescribed number of hire instalments have been paid the customer has an option to purchase the goods for a purely nominal sum. For many years the courts looked only at the legal form of the relationship and saw the company as the sole and complete owner of the goods, but more recently they have recognised the reality of the

---

5. 8th Report, Cmnd 2977, para 164, following the approach of the courts under the earlier legislation the Larceny Act 1916, *Stamp v. United Dominions Trust Ltd* [1967] 1 All ER 251 C.A.

6. cf. comment to *R v. Pemberton* [1983] Crim. L.R. 121.

7. Criminal Justice Act 1982 sect. 67.

situation: the hire purchase company needs the goods only as a security for the outstanding balance of the purchase price.[8] If the goods are worth more (for instance, because a large deposit or a high proportion of the payments have been made), the difference, in some senses at least, 'belongs'[9] to the customer. One important context, where this is the case, is where the customer stops paying and the company wishes to recover the goods. It will only be able to get a civil court order for delivery of the goods if it is prepared to pay an allowance for the customer's 'equity' – the difference between the value of the goods and the outstanding balance of the purchase price.[10]

If hirers who stop paying are also dishonest, and are convicted of theft or a like offence, should the criminal court make a restitution order without similarly giving credit for the customer's equity? We think not. The purpose of a restitution order is to restore the *status quo ante*, and this is done by making the type of order a civil court would make. Of course, the offender is *ex hypothesi* dishonest and his offence may merit some penalty in addition to restoration of the *status quo ante*. Whatever other penalty the Court may impose there is no justification for in effect paying the fine to the finance company and making it better off than if the offence had not been committed. We do not think that the making of this calculation would cause the criminal court any great difficulty.

The second situation where a restitution order may leave the owner better off than before the offence is where the goods have been improved. Again this is a problem which has concerned the civil law system. By the Torts (Interference with Goods) Act 1977 a person who improves goods in the honest but mistaken belief that he has a good title to them can insist on being paid an allowance to reflect the increase in value of the goods before being made to hand them back to their true owner.[11] Parliament accepted that this could mean that an owner might be forced to pay for improvements that he did not want, but if his goods were worth more as a result, and the improver was honest, it was thought that this was a lesser evil than leaving the

---

8. *Wickham Holdings Ltd v. Brooke House Motors Ltd* [1967] 1 All ER 117 and *Belvoir Finance Co. Ltd v. Stapleton* [1971] 1 Q.B. 210 disapproving of *United Dominions Trust (Commercial) Ltd v. Parkway Motors Ltd* [1955] 2 All ER 557 to the contrary.

9. We put the words 'belong' and 'equity' in quotation marks because strictly speaking, the hire purchase is not a mortgagee and the hirer has no equity. However the approach to the creditor's remedies discussed in the text makes the parties' relationship closely analogous.

10. Torts (Interference with Goods) Act 1977 sect. 3(6). Alternatively the court will deduct an equivalent amount for the damages that the hirer is ordered to pay. See cases cited in note 8.

11. 1977 Act sect. 3(7) and sect. 6.

improver without any consolation.[12] It will be seen that the *dishonest* improver can make no claim. Consequently, when making a restitution order against a defendant (who is by definition dishonest) the criminal court need not consider improvements. However, restitution orders can be made for instance, against *bona fide* purchasers from a thief under sect. 28(1)(a). The criminal court ought then, like the civil court, to consider how much the improvements have increased the value of the goods and to make a restitution order conditional on an allowance for this being paid. If sect.28(1)(a) does not presently enable them to do this, it ought to be amended.

In a third respect, the beneficiaries of a criminal restitution order may be in a better position than if they had taken civil proceedings. A civil court will rarely insist that the defendant deliver up goods that have been wrongly taken or detained, especially where they are ordinary articles of commerce with no special value or interest to the plaintiff.[13] Normally the Court will give the defendant the option to deliver the goods or to pay their value as damages.[14] In principle where the goods have no special value to the victim, there seems no good reason why the defendant should not be able to discharge the restitution order by opting to pay their value. However we can see why, given the proven or admitted dishonesty of these defendants and their often doubtful means, the option should almost always be exercised by actual payment rather than by a promise or undertaking to pay.

(3) The power to order payment of a monetary equivalent

The powers to order restitution in the Theft Act 1968 of course preceded the present power to order compensation in the Powers of Criminal Courts Act 1973. The courts could make compensation orders in 1968 (under the Forfeiture Act 1870), but only in much more restricted circumstances (see chapter 2). Now under sect. 35 of the 1973 Act the court would clearly be able to order the defendant to pay 'a sum not exceeding the value of the . . . goods . . . to any person who if those goods were in the possession of the person convicted would be entitled to recover them from him' (1968 Act sect. 28(1)(c). We agree with the submission we received from the Association of Chief Police Officers

---

12. Cf. *Greenwood v. Bennett* [1973] 1 QB 195; the Law Reform Committee 18th Report, Cmnd 4774; and Goff and Jones, *The Law of Restitution*, 2nd edn., pp. 111–14.
13. *Whiteley Ltd v. Hilt* [1918] 2 KB 808, 819; *Howard E. Perry Ltd v. British Railways Board* [1980] 2 All ER 579, 586; cf. J.K. McLeod, 'Restitution under the Theft Act 1968' [1968] Crim. L.R. 577.
14. Torts (Interference with Goods) Act 1977 sect. 3(2) (b).

that this overlap is an example of the need to codify the courts' powers which in this context could be adequately done by repealing sect. 28(1)(c).

One difference between the two powers appears to be that the defendant's means must be considered before making an order under sect. 35, but need not be taken into account in making one under sect. 28(1)(c).[15] We can appreciate that the defendant's means are irrelevant where the stolen property or its proceeds can be identified, i.e. where an order is made under sect. 28(1)(a) or 28(1)(b). The law can reasonably say that but for the wrong doing, the defendant would not have had the use of that which is taken from him by the order. But sect. 28(1)(c) is different: it is intended for use where the goods or their proceeds cannot be identified. Alternatively, it might be used where the goods are returned to the owner in a damaged state. In all these cases the Court is ordering the defendant to pay compensation to the owner out of his own money and in doing so it ought to take account of the defendant's financial ability. The sub-section does now limit the court to ordering compensation out of money taken from the defendant at the time of his apprehension, but for two reasons this is less satisfactory than taking account of his means. Firstly, the defendant's possession of money says nothing about his obligations. He may have been arrested on his way to pay the rent or do the shopping. A restitution order may properly require some sacrifice on the part of the defendant, but we think that the Court ought to weigh the competing needs of the defendant and his other creditors or dependants just as it will do before making a compensation order in favour of a victim of violence or criminal damage. The second criticism of this limitation is the converse: the court ought to be able to order a defendant with adequate means to pay compensation whether money is in his possession or not at the time of his arrest. 'Possession' has been given a wide meaning, so that a defendant in possession of a key to a safe deposit box was held to be in possession of the contents of the box at the time of his arrest.[16] However, an order would not have been made under sect. 28(1)(c) if the money had instead been credited to an account at the bank. It would have been recognised in assessing the defendant's means for a compensation order under sect. 35. We conclude that the practice under sect. 35 of focusing on the defendant's means is preferable and the different approach under sect.

---

15. See for example *R v. Lewis* [1975] Crim. L.R. 353.
16. *R v. Ferguson.*

28(1)(c) is not a reason for retaining that power.[17]

If the court has judged that the defendant can and ought to pay compensation, using money taken on his arrest to satisfy the order is a quick and convenient means of enforcement. However, it is equally useful for all the other financial orders which a court may make. Magistrates' courts do have a power to order compensation and fines to be paid in this way.[18] There seems to be no equivalent power in the crown court but this may be because the crown court must remit enforcement of its orders to the defendants' local magistrates' court. It is sufficient for the latter court to be able to apply money taken from him on arrest for this purpose.

(4) Competing claims by victims

The effect of an order under sect. 28 is to transfer possession from the defendant or a third party to the person 'entitled to recover them'. The essential issue for the court where there are competing claims by victims should be 'which of them has the best right to possess the goods?' Normally (but not always) this will be the owner. If goods are stolen from a pawnbroker, the pawnbroker rather than the owner is the person 'entitled to recover' them. If a car has been left at a garage to be repaired and is waiting for collection at the time that it is taken, the garage will have a lien over the car for its charges. Again, the garage is entitled to possession of the car until the charges have been paid. In both these examples, the owner gave up his right of possession. The position is rather more complex if a thief has dealt with the goods. Generally the Court ought not to restore the goods to people who subsequently bought or acquired them; since the thief had no title, they have no claim. Consequently, magistrates rightly refused to make an order in favour of a jeweller to whom a stolen ring had been given for examination.[19] Occasionally, though, a thief *can* give rights. A hotel, for instance, has a lien over its visitors' goods for its charges. This extends even to stolen goods (as long as the hotel was ignorant of their origins). Thus the Ritz Hotel was able to recover a

---

17. Similarly the power now in sect. 28(3) to order the defendant to pay compensation to a *bona fide* purchaser who is ordered to restore the goods to the original owner would be better placed in the sections of the Powers of Criminal Courts Act 1973 which provide for compensation orders. Under sect. 35 as presently enacted, the duped third party would only be able to obtain compensation if the thief or handler were also charged with obtaining money by deception from him. For the same reasons as are given in the text, this power should also be subject to the defendant's means.

18. Magistrates Courts Act 1980 sect. 81(8) and sect. 150.

19. *Raymond Lyons v. Metropolitan Police Commissioner* [1975] 1 All ER 335.

ring which had been left by a thief in their room and to use it to reduce his unpaid bill.[20] These last two cases were decided under the Police (Property) Act 1897 which gives magistrates in simple cases jurisdiction to decide who should have property in the possession of the police. Although that Act speaks of the court ordering delivery 'to the person appearing . . . to be the owner thereof', the latter case shows that courts can and should look rather at who has the best right to possess the goods.

In *R v. Thibeault*[21] the competing claims were by owners of different stolen goods. The thief had accumulated the proceeds of his offences to buy other goods. The Court of Appeal held that there was no present power in sect. 28 to order the sale of these other goods and the distribution of the proceeds *pro rata*. We favour amending sect. 28 to allow the court to do just this.

(5) Practice

The Court can act of its own motion to restore the goods themselves (under sect. 28(1)(a)) or to order payment of a monetary equivalent (under sect. 28(1)(c)). But an application is necessary before the proceeds of stolen goods can be restored. The application may be made by the victim or by the police or prosecution but if no application is made, the Court has no jurisdiction.[22] The requirement of an application has been justified on the grounds that the Court ought not itself to embark on difficult questions of tracing,[23] but we think this a rather arbitrary line. Compensation may also raise difficult issues; at present the 'clear case' restriction ensures that the over-burdened criminal courts do not have to spend time on complicated cases: until the work-load of the criminal courts is under control a similar restriction would, no doubt, be applied in the case of restoration of the proceeds of stolen goods. We would recommend abolishing the requirement of an application in cases falling within sect. 28(1)(b).

Under the Police (Property) Act 1897, an application or a complaint is necessary. This seems sensible since the procedure, unlike that under sect. 28, is not dependent on a conviction. It may be initiated when no prosecution is launched, often on acquittal, or some time after sentence. Some initiating process is therefore necessary, and we agree that the Court should not be responsible for setting this in train. There has recently emerged an unmeritorious distinction between the methods of invoking the Court's jurisdiction. Magistrates cannot

---

20. *Marsh v. Commer. of Police for the Metropolis* [1944] 2 All ER 392.
21. *R v. Thibeault* [1983] Crim. L.R. 102.
22. *Ibid.*
23. Griew, *The Theft Acts 1968 and 1978*, 4th edn., para 16–05.

award costs if an application is made, but can if the case has been started by way of complaint.[24] The police should be treated in the same way as interpleaders, who, in civil proceedings, disavow any personal interest in property and declare their willingness to hand it over to whomsoever the court directs.[25] They are not then responsible for the costs incurred in deciding who is the rightful owner. Immunity from costs in the civil context depends on complete passivity. If the police oppose the order, even if only 'in order to assist the court to assess the validity of the claim or claims made to the ownership of the property', the successful claimant ought normally to have his costs paid, though in these circumstances they ought to come from central funds.[26]

24. *R v. Uxbridge Justices ex parte Commissioner of Police for the Metropolis* [1981] 3 All ER 129 C.A.
25. Rules of Supreme Court Order 17.
26. In this situation, Sir Stanley Rees thought that no order for costs should be made against the police. Since an order that costs be paid out of central funds would require amending legislation, that possibility was not canvassed before this court. *R v. Uxbridge JJ* at p. 141.

8 Forfeiture

We have defined 'forfeiture' as referring to the Court's power to take property immediately connected with an offence. We have contrasted this with 'confiscation' of the profit or proceeds of the offence and 'restitution' of stolen property to its rightful owner.

(1) General powers of forfeiture

The criminal courts now have a general power of forfeiture under sect. 43 of Powers of Criminal Courts Act 1973. This provides:

(1) Where a person is convicted of an offence punishable on indictment with imprisonment for a term of two years or more and the court by or before which he is convicted is satisfied that any property which was in his possession or under his control at the time of his apprehension –
   (a) has been used for the purpose of committing, or facilitating the commission of, any offence; or
   (b) was intended by him to be used for that purpose;
   The court may make an order under this section in respect of that property.

(2) Facilitating the commission of an offence shall be taken . . . to include the taking of any steps after it has been committed for the purpose of disposing of any property to which it relates or of avoiding apprehension or detention and references . . . to an offence punishable with imprisonment shall be construed without regard to any prohibition or restriction imposed by or under any enactment on the imprisonment of young offenders.

(3) An order under this section shall operate to deprive the offender of his rights, if any, in the property to which it relates, and the property shall (if not already in their possession) be taken into the possession of the police.

This legislation supplemented and did not replace specific powers of forfeiture attached to particular offences. Further specific powers have been added since 1973. Consequently the full powers of the criminal courts can only be gathered from statutes as diverse as the Vagrancy Act 1824, the Obscene Publications Acts 1959–64, the Deer Act 1963, the Lotteries and Amusements Act 1967 and the Forgery and Conterfeiting Act 1981.

(2) Specific powers of forteiture

There is a good reason for the continued use of specific powers where they relate to offences which are committed by the possession of a prohibited article. Thus the Import of Live Fish (England and Wales)

Act 1980 allows the government to control the importing or keeping of non-native fish which might compete with, displace, prey on or harm the habitat of any freshwater fish, shellfish or salmon in England and Wales. It is an offence to import or keep prohibited fish or to do so without a prescribed licence. On conviction any fish in respect of which the offence was committed must be forfeited (sect. 3(3)). It would be clumsy to incorporate provisions of this type into a general power such as sect. 43 of the 1973 Act.

Some statutes which deal with prohibited articles allow a much wider power of forfeiture. Sect. 27(1) of the Misuse of Drugs Act 1971 for instance says,

the court by or before which a person is convicted of an offence under this Act may order anything shown to the satisfaction of the court to relate to the offence to be forfeited.

To the extent that this allows the forfeiture of the illegal drugs themselves, it falls into the category just considered where a separate forfeiture power can be justified. Clearly, though, sect. 27 is wider. It has been used to forfeit cars in which drugs have been transported and money paid for drugs.[1] In this wider sense, its function is indistinguishable from the general power of forfeiture in sect. 43 of the 1973 Act and we can see no good reason for the overlap. The same principles, which we discuss below, ought to apply but the present difference in wording may lead to anomalous results; for instance, sect. 43 could possibly be used to forfeit property intended to be used by conspirators, while the House of Lords in *R v. Cuthbertson*[2] held that sect. 27 could not be used against defendants convicted of conspiring to break the 1971 Act. Consequently, here and in other statutes,[3] which at present use the same or similar wording, we would recommend that the specific power be confined to forfeiture or prohibited articles and that in relation to other property, the general power in sect. 43 should be used.

(3) Forfeiture without conviction

There are rare cases where the danger to the public from the circulation of noxious articles is sufficiently grave that they should be liable to seizure even prior to a criminal conviction. For instance, under powers conferred by the Forgery and Counterfeiting Act 1981[4] counterfeit coins and forged banknotes may be forfeited by magistrates acting in a quasi-criminal capacity. For these powers to be

1. For example, *R v. Lidster* [1976] Crim. L.R. 80; *R v. Menocal* [1979] 2 All ER 510 (though the order was there quashed because of a procedural defect).
2. [1981] A.C. 470.
3. For example, Forfeiture and Counterfeiting Act 1981 sect. 24(3).
4. Sects. 7 and 24.

exercisable the object must come within the prescribed class and forfeiture must be conducive to the public interest.[5] Owners have an opportunity to intervene and show cause why the order should not be made. Owners appear to carry the burden of proof and they have no formal right to receive notice of the application.[6]

It was by analogy with such inherently vicious goods that obscene publications were first subjected to forfeiture in 1857.[7] Destruction orders are made by magistrates, but as they exercise this jurisdiction in a quasi-criminal capacity, the sole issue is whether the items should be forfeited. The owners (the publisher, author or any other person through whose hands they had passed)[8] can argue why the order should not be made. If unsuccessful they can be subjected to no greater penalty than the loss of their property.

Such forfeiture proceedings are sometimes referred to as *in rem*: it is said that the allegedly obscene article or other property is on trial not its owner or possessor.[9] A comparison can be drawn with the old law of deodand (see chapter 2). In the United States, this notion is highlighted by the very title of the action (for example *U.S. v. One Book called 'Ulysses'* 5.F. Supp. 182; *'Memoirs of a Lady of Pleasure' v. Massachusetts* 383 U.S. 463). But this personification of property is sophistry. Property does not exist in a vacuum. As Chief Baron Parker said in 1766[10] 'goods as goods cannot offend, forfeit . . . pay duties or the like but [only] men whose goods they are'. Forfeiture entails loss of property rights and is as much a penalty as a fine. Indeed, in the case of obscenity, the destruction of a large stock of obscene materials can involve a loss which exceeds many times over the maximum fines which the magistrates could impose in their criminal capacity.[11] It may be that the circulation or use of obscene publications, counterfeit coins or forged banknotes has to be stopped irrespective of the criminal intention of those who possess or own them, but in effect a civil forfeiture provision creates a strict liability criminal offence for which the sole penalty is loss of the property concerned.

The penal function of these powers is even more apparent where the items subject to forfeiture are not inherently harmful but have been

5. *Ibid.*, sect. 7(2) and 24(2).
6. Contrast those whom the Customs Commissioners know to be owners of seized property. They must be given a formal notification of their rights. Customs and Excise Management Act 1979, Sched 3, para 12.
7. Obscene Publications Act 1857. See Geoffrey Robertson, *Obscenity* (Weidenfeld and Nicolson, 1979), pp. 26–33.
8. Obscene Publications Act 1959 sect. 3.
9. *Calero-Toledo v. Pearson Yacht Leasing Co.* 416 U.S. 663, 686 citing *Goldsmith-Grant Co. v. U.S.* 254 U.S. 505, 510 (1921).
10. *Mitchell v. Torup* Parker 227 at 236, 145 E.R. 764, 767 citing *Sheppard v. Gosnold* Vaughan, 159, 172, 124 E.R. 1018, 1024 (CP 1673).
11. Robertson, *Obscentity*, p. 105.

associated with a criminal offence. There is nothing dangerous *per se*, for instance, about a ship which has been used to carry contraband. In 1978,[12] the United States extended its powers of civil forfeiture to cover the proceeds of drug offences (see further chapter 3). Again, property such as this is clearly forfeited as a way of punishing its owners.

We find this concept of quasi-criminal forfeiture troubling. It can too easily be used as a way of penalising criminal conduct without the safeguards of the ordinary criminal process. Of course, the defendant may well view the instigation of these forfeiture proceedings as the lesser of two evils and be content to risk the seizure of his property rather than have his liberty put in jeopardy. Few owners bother to challenge the lawfulness of customs' seizures.[13] This is not always so with other forfeitures. Many publishers have complained that the forfeiture procedure under the Obscene Publications Act deprives them of a jury's verdict on whether their books really are likely to deprave and corrupt and are therefore 'obscene' or whether they are defensible in the public good.[14] In 1964, the Solicitor General gave Parliament an undertaking which was understood to mean that a publisher faced with a forfeiture proceeding could insist on being tried for the parallel criminal offence.[15] This seems sensible. Property inimical to the public good can be seized and, if no one comes forward, destroyed; but an objector would be able to insist on either challenging the lawfulness of the seizure in forfeiture proceedings or in a full dress criminal trial with its attendant risks and rights. On only one occasion has a publisher been allowed to exercise this option.[16] On many others the forfeiture proceedings have continued despite the declared preference of the publisher for a criminal trial.[17]

The purpose of forfeiture orders of this sort is to take out of circulation goods that are inherently dangerous or contrary to the

12. 21 U.S.C. 881.
13. Commissioners of Customs and Excise Memorandum no. 3 to the Keith Committee on Enforcement Powers, April 1980.
14. Robertson, *Obscenity*, p. 105.
15. 'In the absence of special circumstances and if satisfactory evidence of the offence is available, the ordinary policy of the Director of Public Prosecutions will be to proceed against the publishers by way of prosecution; first where an article has been seized under a warrant from a retailer or printer and the publisher, before the case is brought before the justice under sect. 3 of the 1959 Act, indicates his intention to continue publishing whatever the result of the forfeiture proceedings; and, secondly, where enquiries are being made about an article which the prosecution considers to be prima facie obscene and the publisher indicates his determination to publish, and to continue to publish, in circumstances which would constitute a criminal offence.' Sir Peter Rawlinson Q.C., Solicitor-General, Hansard, 7 July 1964, col. 296.
16. Concerning *Last Exit to Brooklyn* in 1967. Cf. Robertson, *Obscenity*, p. 107.
17. *Ibid.*, p. 105.

public interest. There is little dispute that such orders should be within a court's competence, though there is, of course, vigorous public debate about whether particular types of goods, for instance obscene publications, are sufficiently harmful to justify subjecting them to the possibility of such orders. We think that such orders should clearly be retained but believe that the owner should always have the right to insist that he be put on a criminal trial before suffering the loss of his goods rather than merely contesting the forfeiture proceedings.

(4) Forfeiture as crime prevention

Another purpose of forfeiture powers is crime prevention. Sect. 43 allows the forfeiture of property which 'was intended by [the defendant] to be used [for the purpose of committing or facilitating the commission of any offence]'. Where the property has already been used for the purpose of committing or facilitating the commission of an offence, the court's motive in making a forfeiture order may be to prevent a repetition of the offence. Thus in *R v. Attarde*[18] the court forfeited the defendant's car, which had an additional petrol pump fitted in order to be able to siphon fuel from other cars. The Advisory Council on the Penal System whose recommendation prompted the enactment of sect. 43 intended that crime prevention should be its main purpose.[19]

In line with that purpose it might be argued that the Court's powers of forfeiture ought not to be confined to forfeiting property connected with offences of which the defendant was convicted but should extend to other property that the defendant might intend to use for lawful purposes. Very occasionally, a statute allows this. For instance, under the Firearms Act 1968, the Court may order the seizure of any guns or ammunition in the convicted person's possession, not only those that formed the basis of an offence of which the defendant was convicted.[20] It has been argued,[21] that sect. 43 presently gives the court a wider power to do the same since it speaks of property which has been used or was intended for the purpose of committing or facilitating *any* offence. However, the great majority of the submissions thought that this would not be a welcome interpretation. Forfeiture should relate only to offences of which the defendant was convicted or asked to be taken into consideration.

---

18. [1975] Crim. L.R. 729.
19. Sub-committee (chaired by Lady Wootton) of the Advisory Council on the Penal System, Non-Custodial and Semi-Custodial Penalties (1970), paras 145–9.
20. Firearms Act 1968 sect. 52.
21. D.A. Thomas, *Principles of Sentencing*, 2nd edn. p. 335.

(5) Forfeiture as an additional penalty

Forfeiture has also been used for a third purpose; as simply another penalty. This is most clearly the case where a car, which the defendant used to travel to or from the scene of the crime, is forfeited. The Court of Appeal held[22] that a forfeiture order may then be made though the car has not been modified (like that in *Attarde*). We agree that this may be an appropriate type of penalty, but we think it would be wrong always to add forfeiture as an additional penalty because of some mystical connection with the wrong-doing (as with medieval deodand – see chapter 2). This type of forfeiture is in effect a fine *in specie*, and ought to be considered as such. Consequently it ought not to be combined with other penalties if the total effect would be too severe. In *R v. Thompson*[23] the defendant obtained £8800 by pretending to an insurance company that his car (worth that sum) had been stolen. He received a fifteen-month suspended sentence, a fine of £5000 and was ordered to forfeit the car. The Court of Appeal reduced the suspended sentence to nine months and quashed the forfeiture order because it regarded the cumulative effect of the orders as too onerous. Alternatively, as in *Lidster*, the Court has said that the other penalties should reflect the loss of the forfeited goods.

A second corollary of using forfeiture as a penalty is that the court should have regard to the defendant's means. Thus in *R v. Taverner*[24] the defendant was ordered to forfeit his car after being convicted of handling stolen goods which had been conveyed in the car. The Court of Appeal quashed the order because the car had been purchased by the defendant out of compensation for an accident which had left him handicapped. He could not have afforded another car. The further penalties of a twelve-month suspended sentence and a £100 fine were considered sufficient.

In these cases, we think consideration should be given to allowing the defendant to pay a pecuniary penalty to the value of the goods instead of losing his property. This would, in effect, make the forfeiture order security for a fine. Courts cannot do this under the present law,[25] but a change would be desirable. If a car is forfeited, expenses will be incurred in storing and selling it. Its value to the defendant in terms of convenience or sentiment may be greater than what it would fetch at a public auction. In the United States, the courts have similarly adapted powers of confiscation to allow the defendant to 'buy back' the property (see chapter 4). The only diffi-

22. For example, *R v. Lidster*.
23. (1977) 66 Cr. App. R. 130.
24. 4 April 1974, unreported; but see Sweet & Maxwell's, *Current Sentencing Practice*, J 4.4(b).
25. *R v. Kingston-upon-Hull Justices ex parte Hartung* (1980) 72 Cr. App. R. 26.

culty would be in calculating an appropriate amount for the alternative penalty, but this would not seem to be insuperable. The Court would also have to retain a discretion to declare that its forfeiture order was not simply penal, but intended either to remove prohibited goods from circulation or as a means of crime prevention and so deprive the defendant of the 'buy back option'.

(6) Changes to the general forfeiture power

(a)   The type of property

The property must have firstly been used or intended for use for the purpose of committing or facilitating the commission of the offence. Even though forfeiture is now used as a penalty as well as a means of crime prevention, we think that the first restriction is still justified. If the Court imposes a fine as an alternative penalty, distress or civil judgment powers may eventually be used as means of enforcing payment. Thus, in due course, any part of the defendant's property, and not just that connected with the offence, may be seized in satisfaction of the debt. We agree, though, with the present principle that summary enforcement should be confined to property associated with the offence in one of the ways set out in sect. 43.

Property can only be forfeited under sect. 43 at present if it was also found in the possession or control of the defendant at the time of his arrest. This restriction can lead to anomalies. In *R v. Hinde*[26] the defendant was observed close to his car shortly after he had burgled a house. The car was seized, but the man escaped and was arrested four days later. The Court of Appeal ruled that the car had not been in his possession at the time of his apprehension and therefore could not be forfeited.

The restriction may have been based on a desire not to extend the police powers of seizure, but this justification dissolves if the police have a right to seize the property for some other reason or, as in *Hinde*, on some other occasion. The police can often seize property which they have reasonable grounds to believe will be needed as evidence and property which satisfies the first restriction (having been used or intended for committing or facilitating an offence) will almost always come within that category. For these reasons we think that sect. 43 ought to apply to property which has been lawfully seized at any time by the police or other authorities. This would also mean that sect. 43 could be used where the defendant is not apprehended but appears at court in answer to a summons.

26. (1977) 64 Cr. App. R. 213.

(b) Type of offence

Sect. 43 presently applies only to an offence which is punishable on indictment with at least two years' imprisonment. We agree with the representations that were made to us that this is the wrong way to circumscribe the power. Since the power has become a means of imposing a penalty, we think the proper focus should be the value of the property. A court should be able to make a forfeiture order if the value of the property does not exceed the maximum fine for the offence. If the defendant is also fined or subjected to a compensation order, the financial penalties in total should not exceed the maximum fine (by analogy with the present limit on compensation orders in sect. 35(5) of the Magistrates Courts Act 1980).

(c) Extent of forfeiture

Under sect. 43 the court (1) forfeits the offender's rights and (2) directs the police to hold possession of the goods pending any claims by third parties. Third parties can recover their property if they can show that they did not consent to the defendant's possession or if they did not know and had no reason to suspect the defendant's use of or plans for their property (1973 Act sect. 43(4)(h); see also chapter 12).

We agree that forfeiture needs to be more extensive where the very possession of the goods is an offence. This is a further reason why we favour the retention of specific forfeiture powers in such cases. However other property related to drug offences should be dealt with in accordance with sect. 43: that is, the Court should forfeit the defendant's interest and hand it over to, or leave it in the possession of, the police. Third party claimants who can establish their lack of knowledge or consent should then be able to recover it. At present sect. 27(2) of the Misuse of Drugs Act 1971 simply gives third parties an opportunity to appear and be heard before the sentencing court makes its order. This is less satisfactory, firstly because there is a greater chance that some third parties will not learn of the proceedings until after the order has been made and (as we would recommend, see chapter 12) advertised. Secondly, the unfettered discretion in sect. 27 of the 1971 Act is less preferable to setting out as in sect. 43 the criteria by which third parties can establish a right to recover their property.

The Court of Appeal in *R v. Troth*[27] held that, as with compensation cases, forfeiture should only be ordered in clear cases. In that case a lorry was jointly owned by the defendant and a business

---

27. (1979) 71 Cr. App. R. 1.

partner. A forfeiture order was held to be inapt. In the chapters on compensation and confiscation we have elaborated our critique of the 'clear case' test.

Part Three

9 Pre-trial restraint

This topic lies at the heart of any increased use of forfeiture, confiscation or compensation by the courts. At present there are occasions when the defendant in a criminal case does voluntarily disclose his assets, to a greater extent than would be revealed in any event by police enquiries. This may happen typically when (i) the defendant is in peril of being sent to prison, but (ii) there is some prospect that the court may be persuaded to impose a fine or compensation order rather than an immediate sentence of imprisonment, and (iii) the defendant has means which would enable a realistic financial penalty to be enforced promptly. Needless to say the objective of avoiding an immediate sentence of imprisonment is not always achieved. A defendant's legal advisers will rightly be wary of suggesting a course which may result in his losing both his money and his liberty. Such occasions are consequently rare. In all other cases involving serious crime, a defendant has no incentive to disclose his assets or to maintain them in a form where they can be reached by the courts. Generally he has a sound motive for not doing so. Moreover a lawful method of putting assets that comprise or can be converted into money beyond the reach of the courts is ready to hand since the abolition of exchange control restrictions.

(1) Restraint of defendant's assets in civil proceedings

(a) Mareva *injunctions*
The pre-trial measures in civil cases which we have considered are three. First, there is the *Mareva* injunction, by which a person is temporarily restrained from removing either specified assets or his assets generally outside the jurisdiction, or from disposing of them within the jurisdiction. This is a creature of recent but rapid growth in the civil law. It may be, and on occasion is, sought by a plaintiff whose cause of action is founded on criminal behaviour on the part of the defendant.[1] In such a case it is not unknown for the plaintiff to seek assistance from the police, and even to be encouraged by the police to apply for an injunction. But the police cannot themselves apply, save in limited circumstances which we shall presently consider.

1. *A v. C* [1981] Q.B. 956.

(b) Orders for defendants to disclose the whereabouts of their assets

The second and third measures which we have considered are ancillary to a *Mareva* injunction. The second is an order for discovery of documents relating to assets, or an order that the defendant disclose on affidavit where his assets are. There is jurisdiction to make such an order.[2] Whilst a *Mareva* injunction is almost invariably sought *ex parte*, because the very object to be achieved might be lost if the defendant were warned that the order were about to be made, there is usually no reason why the defendant should not be notified of such an application for discovery. He will, after all, have to be notified of the order before he can comply with it. Such orders are frequently sought *ex parte*, but rarely granted except on a summons. They differ also from a *Mareva* injunction in that it is the defendant alone who is, in general, concerned to comply with an order for discovery. The great advantage of a *Mareva* injunction is that notice of it can be given to banks or other upright persons who are thought to hold assets of the defendant; any person who with notice assists a breach of the injunction is guilty of contempt of court.[3] Enforcement of the order is thus not wholly dependent on the desire of the defendant (who may have a fleeting connection with this country) to avoid imprisonment. On the other hand, in the case of an order for discovery, enforcement is in general wholly dependent on the co-operation of the defendant. These general observations about the practice do not apply where a plaintiff seeks discovery of documents relating to assets from a third party, as in *Bankers Trust Company v. Shapira*.[4] In such a case enforcement of the order is not dependent on the will of the defendant. Nor does the defendant have to be notified before application for such an order is made.

(c) Search of defendant's premises

We turn to the third measure, the *Anton Piller* order.[5] This is an order that the defendant do permit representatives of the plaintiff to enter the defendant's premises and there to search for and remove documents or other property that would be evidence relevant to the plaintiff's case. Such an order is a strong measure in a civil case, and is rarely used; but it is made *ex parte*. Although born and bred in cases about piracy of intellectual property, it has been used in a matrimonial dispute[6] and, we are told, in other classes of case. It does not, in the main, suffer from the defect that enforcement depends on the will of

---

2. *Bekhor Ltd v. Bilton* [1981] 2 WLR 601.
3. *Z Ltd v. A–Z* [1982] QB 558.
4. [1980] 1 WLR 1274.
5. *Anton Piller KG v. Manufacturing Processes Ltd.* [1976] Ch. 55.
6. *Emanuel v. Emanuel* [1982] 1 W.L.R. 669.

the defendant. But it has given rise to problems about the privilege against self-incrimination. That difficulty has now been dealt with, as regards intellectual property cases, by sect. 72 of the Supreme Court Act 1981, which removes the privilege, but makes evidence so obtained inadmissible in criminal proceedings for a related offence.

(2) Pre-trial restraint of assets in criminal proceedings: the current position

To what extent are these measures presently available to the police? The general rule is that the police have no power to retain property of a defendant in a criminal case (not being property which will be relevant evidence at the trial) in anticipation that an order may be made by way of compensation or forfeiture.[7] The result is that the police have, on occasion, had to hand over to persons awaiting trial very large sums of money, which were neither required as evidence nor arguably the property of anyone other than the defendants; when later those defendants have been convicted, it has not been apparent that the money was still within reach of the courts.

There are three reported cases where an injunction has been granted pending a criminal trial – *West Mercia Constabulary v. Wagener*[8], *Chief Constable of Kent v. V*[9] and *Chief Constable of Hampshire v. A*[9a] – and others that are not reported. We take the present law to be that the police may obtain an injunction freezing a bank account or some other asset in the hands of a defendant if, but only if, the asset is arguably the property of a victim of crime, whether because it was itself criminally obtained by the defendant or represents the proceeds of property so obtained. Such an order is not truly a *Mareva* injunction at all, since it is founded on proprietary right rather than on a desire to preserve assets so that some future monetary orders may be enforced. The only innovation in those cases, in our view, was that proceedings were brought by the police rather than by the person or persons whose property had been criminally obtained.

As to discovery and *Anton Piller* orders, as the books show, these have not so far been granted to the police in civil proceedings. As part of their powers of search, with or without a warrant, the police frequently discover evidence as to assets of the defendant. But they cannot presently search for such assets alone, independently of any enquiry as to whether a crime has been committed by the defendant. Nor under the Bankers Books Evidence Act 1879 do we suppose that

---

7. *Malone v. Metropolitan Police Commissioner* [1980] Q.B. 49.
8. [1982] 1 WLR 127.
9. [1982] 3 All ER 36.
9a. *The Times*, 3 March 1984.

they can apply for an order to inspect the defendant's bank account solely for the purpose of detecting assets which might later be used to pay a fine or compensation order. A further difficulty is that there must be an existing legal proceeding before an order can be made.

(3) Proposed powers in criminal proceedings

We consider that there is a powerful case for changing the law to some extent, subject to appropriate safeguards. There does not appear to be much logic in allowing the victim, by an application in a civil suit, to restrain a defendant's bank account, so that it will still be available when an order is made for the payment of damages, but denying a similar right to the state which may later seek to enforce a fine or, as we hope, in the future confiscation. Furthermore the object of a compensation order is to relieve the victim or victims of the expense and inconvenience of bringing civil proceedings. The state ought, by pre-trial restraint, to be able to ensure that money will be available to enforce a compensation order, just as the victim or victims could in civil proceedings.

We find support for our views in the judgment of Roskill L.J. in *Malone's* case.

If the police require such powers for this purpose – and one can appreciate that in this day and age it might be convenient for them to have them – the police must seek the requisite powers from Parliament – if they can obtain them.[10]

Also Lord Denning M.R., in the *Chief Constable of Kent's* case said:

It seems to me undesirable that, if a thief is found to have a large sum of money in the bank, he should be able to dispose of it completely, send it to a numbered Swiss bank account, or give it to his accomplices, so as to avoid giving compensation to the people he has defrauded.[11]

Slade L.J. was not convinced that this was 'necessarily and unquestionably . . . desirable'.[12]

The American Federal courts have a power of pre-trial restraint in some criminal cases.[13] Thus in *U.S. v. Mannino & Lombardo*[14] an order was made by the United States District Court for the Southern District of New York restraining the defendants from

10. [1980] QB 49, 69.
11. [1982] 3 All ER 36, 42.
12. *Ibid.*, p. 48.
13. 21 U.S.C. 848 and 18 U.S.C. 1961–63.
14. Southern District of New York 1980. The orders are reproduced in 'The Rico Statute; An Overview' prepared by the Research Division of the Secretariat of the Solicitor-General of Canada for the Federal/Provincial Task Force on Enterprise Crime, p. 94.

Selling, assigning, pledging, distributing, or otherwise disposing of any part
of their beneficial interest, direct or indirect, in Habor Racquetball Limited
located in Brooklyn, New York, in property located at 474 Van Sicklen
Avenue, Brooklyn, New York, or in property located at 120 South New
Hampshire Avenue, Atlantic City, New Jersey, without prior approval of this
Court on notice to the United States.

(a) Injunction freezing assets

We consider that the Court should have power to make an interim
order freezing assets if there is a *prima facie* case that the defendant has
committed an indictable offence, and it appears likely that on conviction the Court will consider imposing a fine and/or compensation
or confiscation orders totalling £10,000 or more. The order would
be made by a high court judge in chambers, normally *ex parte*
and at or shortly before the time of arrest of the defendant, upon the
application of the police or prosecuting authority. Where the property
frozen comprises shares in a business or some other asset which
requires interim management, the Court should be able to entrust that
task to a receiver, although we imagine that, initially at any rate, this
power would be rarely exercised. It would be necessary that the Court
should have power to act on an affidavit of information and belief in
making such an order, without requiring direct or any oral evidence of
the offence alleged. The applicant would be required to establish no
more than a *prima facie* case. Cross-examination at this stage would
not in our view be appropriate.

The defendant would, of course, be able to apply to discharge or
vary the order, in particular so that he can realise assets for living
expenses or the costs of his defence. Other safeguards would be
undertakings, either expressed in the order or to be implied in it by
law,

(i)   to notify the defendant of the order within two working days, or as
        soon as practicable thereafter, and

(ii)   to reimburse any third party who has incurred expense in complying
        with the order.

In an appropriate case it would be right to impose an upper
monetary limit in the order – it would be wrong to freeze assets worth
several hundred thousand pounds if a fine, confiscation or compensation are unlikely to exceed £20,000. There should be power to accept a
bond or guarantee, if offered, in substitution for an order which is
discharged.

(b) Compensation if defendant acquitted

A more difficult topic is whether the applicant for the order should be required to give an undertaking in damages to the defendant, as is invariably done in civil cases. We are not aware that such undertakings are commonly enforced. That may be because the practice of requiring such undertakings deters applications save in cases where the plaintiff is likely to succeed at the trial. Nevertheless it must be a serious possibility that a defendant in a criminal case will suffer damage by his assets being frozen, and will claim to be reimbursed on being acquitted at his trial. A defendant who has been held in custody pending trial does not generally receive compensation for the loss of his liberty; but it does not necessarily follow that he should receive no compensation for the freezing of his assets. The best solution, in our view, is to give the trial judge a discretion, where a defendant's assets have been frozen and he is later acquitted, to order either payment of compensation in a stated amount or an enquiry as to the damage suffered. Such a discretion might well be exercised on the same lines as that to order the payment of costs to a defendant; thus compensation would be refused, for example, where the defendant had brought the prosecution on himself, or had been acquitted on a technicality. There would be no need for any express undertakings as to damages from the applicant for the order; the liability to pay it if ordered to do so by the trial judge would be imposed by law. If the case never came to trial because the defendant was not committed, the order would then expire and any application for costs or compensation would be made to a judge in chambers.

(c) Victim's rights against frozen assets
It must be considered whether the victim should have any rights enforceable against assets so frozen. At the least, we think that the victim should be entitled to enter a *caveat* against the discharge of such an order so that he may have time to obtain a *Mareva* injunction himself. There is a case for arguing that the victim should be able to enforce directly any civil judgment he may obtain, against assets frozen by an order in a criminal case.

(d) Compulsory disclosure of whereabouts of assets
We turn to consider the ancillary remedies that are available in a civil case. There is a good deal to be said against any general power to order a defendant accused of crime to disclose where his assets are, or to make discovery of documents relating to his assets. First, the privilege against self-incrimination would have to be preserved; that would not necessarily be achieved by provisions such as are to be found in sect. 31(1) of the Theft Act 1968[15] and sect. 72 of the Supreme Court Act

15. *Khan v. Khan* [1982] 1 W.L.R. 513.

1981, for the information obtained might be used to incriminate the defendant even if his own statement providing that information could not be used against him. Secondly, it might be difficult to enforce such an order with effective sanctions, and in any event it could well be a time-consuming and expensive process to attempt to do so. The defendant, it must be remembered, is assumed to be unwilling to disclose where his assets are unless effectively compelled to do so.

On the other hand if there is no power at all to obtain information as to assets, the *Mareva* injunction could well be a sterile remedy; the defendant's assets may be frozen from arrest until trial, but at the time when he is sentenced nobody will know what they are. We think that the right course is to increase the power of the police or prosecuting authority to obtain information as to specific assets from third parties. The Bankers Books Evidence Act is, as we have said, insufficient for that purpose. The police in the course of their enquiries into suspected crime frequently uncover information as to where the suspected person may have assets. Once a *Mareva* injunction has been obtained freezing those assets, or the defendant's assets generally, they should have wider powers to demand information from third parties who are thought to hold those assets. The civil remedy provided in a case such as *Bankers Trust Company v. Shapira*[16] ought also to be available in a criminal case.

(e) Receiver of restrained assets

The administration of these new powers may require a degree of expertise which is not presently available. We recommend the appointment of an official to supervise them, who might be called the receiver or custodian of property connected with crime. He would occupy a position similar to, or else be subordinate to, the Director of Public Prosecutions. His functions would be;

(1) to investigate the assets of persons suspected of major crime;
(2) to apply for orders such as those discussed above;
(3) to preserve assets that have been frozen, including where necessary the management of a business;
(4) to release, under the supervision of the court, assets for the living expenses of a defendant or the costs of his defence;
(5) to realise and distribute assets upon final disposal of a case.

There should be power in the receiver or custodian to call in accountants to assist him where necessary.

16. See note 4.

(f) No additional powers of search

We do not consider that *Anton Piller* orders should be granted to the police so that they can search a defendant's premises specifically for evidence of assets, as opposed to searching for the purpose of detecting crime. This would involve a considerable infringement on the liberties of the subject. It may also only rarely be necessary, since such information as to the existence of assets as might be obtained is not infrequently uncovered in the course of detection of crime.

10   Criminal bankruptcy

The idea of adapting the process of civil bankruptcy to the system of criminal justice originated in two memoranda of 1965 and 1966 prepared by the Law Society for submission to the Royal Commission on the Penal System. When that body was dissolved in 1966 and replaced by the Advisory Council on the Penal System the proposal was revived in the course of a thorough review of the courts' powers of restitution and compensation,[1] ultimately finding its legislative expression in the Criminal Justice Act 1972.[2]

The Law Society had recommended that certain offences occasioning loss of, or damage to, property that was not the subject of restitution by the offender, should constitute an act of bankruptcy, and that making of a receiving order should be mandatory upon the Registrar of the Bankruptcy Court. It was clearly thought that there was a substantial advantage in basing the proposal on the existing civil bankruptcy system, rather than devising a separate system, with the consequential practical problem of recruiting and training a separate body of skilled staff to operate it. In particular, the use of the established bankruptcy machinery was thought to be more appropriate than to give the task to the police and/or to some new agency, conferring on them extended powers to search and question the criminal 'debtor'. Moreover, the argument was advanced that any experiment in that direction should involve the minimum of change, by adapting existing procedure to the novel form of criminal bankruptcy. Two systems of bankruptcy operating side by side conceived in the same broad outline, but differing only in detail – one criminal and one civil – would be likely to cause confusion. After all, some of those who have currently been subjected to civil bankruptcy were criminals who may or may not have been prosecuted for their crimes. Criminal bankruptcy was thus conceived as a simple engrafting of the civil, onto the criminal process. The idea, moreover, that the criminal courts should develop an entirely separate and novel sanction was either never envisaged or was rejected out of hand, although, as the Cork Committee on Insolvency Law and Practice was to observe in

1. Report on *Reparation by the Offender* (1970) under the chairmanship of Lord Justice Widgery (late Lord Chief Justice).
2. Criminal Justice Act 1972, sect. 1, now contained in Powers of Criminal Courts Act 1973, sect. 39 *et seq.*

1982,[3] the Law Society's proposal and the ensuing legislation was conceptually unsound. Civil bankruptcy, which is entirely dependent on proof of insolvency, was being used to gather in assets of offenders, 'rich or poor, solvent or insolvent, in furtherance of social objectives' unconnected with the distribution of those assets among the offenders' creditors.[4] The proposed scheme may have made little jurisprudential sense. It appeared at least to possess the virtue of pragmatism.

The proposal was designedly made not as a reflection of any new penal philosophy, but to achieve the twin purposes of deterrence and restitution. Criminal bankruptcy, operating from within the framework of the penal system, was, the Council of the Law Society declared, 'more calculated to affect the incidence of future crimes if precedence is given to the deterrent aspect'.[5] As its chief architect, Sir David Napley, observed shortly after its legislative implementation, the experiment was based on three principles: (i) deterrence; (ii) its vigorous pursuit; and (iii) the onus being on the criminal bankrupt to explain his untoward acquisition of wealth.[6]

The emphasis on deterrence was motivated by the desire to bolster existing, but seemingly inadequate, penal sanctions. Criminal bankruptcy was thus perceived, not even as a sanction in its own right and as a viable alternative to custody, or even other non-custodial penalties (monetary or otherwise), but rather as the second dose of a double penalty system appropriate to punish (and inferentially to deter) the professional criminal, much in the way that a professional person who commits crime may suffer both imprisonment (or some other penal sanction) and disciplinary action at the hands of the offender's professional association.[7] Any concept of reducing or obliterating the term of a custodial sentence as a reward for disclosure of the whereabouts of stolen property or its proceeds seemed, to its authors, at the time unlikely to command public acceptance. (Parole had not been introduced at this time.)

Criminal bankruptcy had one other perceived limitation. The habitual small-time criminal, in general, rapidly squanders whatever money comes into his possession. Even if criminal bankruptcy were at all appropriate or feasible in his case, he would be driven further into crime if he were obliged to make reparation to his victims, either directly or indirectly through bankruptcy. On the other hand, the professional criminal is well practised in the art of disposing of his loot

3. Cmnd 8558, 1982 chapter 41, paras 1709–1724, pp. 385–7.
4. *Ibid.*, paras 1711 and 1722, pp. 385 and 381 respectively.
5. Second Memorandum of February 1966, para 2.
6. [1973] Crim. L.R. pp. 31–5.
7. Second Memorandum of February 1966, para 16.

or covering up the trails of his ill-gotten fortune – in short he is a constantly moving target. Since the bankruptcy procedure operates only *ex post facto*, the opportunity for recovery, however, is extremely limited whether or not the offender has possessed substantial funds prior to his arrest.

Little or no thought was given by the authors of the scheme to crucial matters of pre-arrest or even pre-trial restraints on the offender, supposedly because the civil process of bankruptcy itself makes no such provisions. The main, if not exclusive candidate for criminal bankruptcy was, therefore, to be the person who is normally law-abiding, but commits crime in the course of otherwise lawful occupation – the embezzler, the tax fraudsman, and the fraudulent trader. Such an offender is assumed, by virtue of his general adherence to law-abiding behaviour, to be willing to make available the fruits of his delinquency.

Out of the Law Society's proposals came the provisions in the Criminal Justice Act 1972, on an experimental basis, of criminal bankruptcy.[8] They formed part of the package of provisions contained in the recommendations of the Advisory Council on the Penal System's report, *Reparation by the Offender*, published in 1970. That report was largely a survey of a technical area of law relating to compensation and restitution, and merely recommended a tidying-up and strengthening of the existing statutory provisions. The ensuing Act duly extended and rationalised the courts' powers in that regard. The Advisory Council had recognised that effective redress by the offender, however, required not only adequate powers for the courts to order reparation and the machinery for enforcing payment, but also the existence of resources available to the offender out of which payment to the victim could be expected. It recognised that in many cases the profit from the crime is dissipated or salted away long before offenders are brought to trial, and they do not have the wherewithal to make reparation. But, unhelpfully, it made no proposals for countering the practical situation of the inevitable unavailability of financial resources in the possession of the offender. Following the proposals of the Law Society it merely proposed the adaptation of the bankruptcy procedures so as to make it possible, in strictly selected cases, for the authorities to take control of an offender's assets and income after conviction, and distribute a proportion by way of compensation to the victim.

Under sect. 39 of the Powers of Criminal Courts Act 1973, the crown court may make a criminal bankruptcy order where it appears

8. The provisions are now contained in Powers of Criminal Courts Act 1973 sect. 39, *et seq*. and Sched 2.

that, as a result of offences of which a person has been convicted or had taken into consideration, loss or damage exceeding in the aggregate £15,000 has been suffered by one or more persons known to the court.[9] The effect of the order is to make available the machinery of civil bankruptcy administration for the recovery of the money. A criminal bankruptcy order is an additional penalty and not a sanction in its own right and may be combined with any other disposal except a compensation order. The order is unique in bankruptcy law in that it involves proceedings independently of any state of insolvency of the debtor. The limit of £15,000 may be altered by statutory instrument, but despite inflation, no such alteration has yet been made. Where an order is made it is the duty of the Official Petitioner (whose functions are exclusively vested in the Director of Public Prosecutions) to consider whether it is in the public interest that he should present a bankruptcy petition.[10] If the Official Petitioner presents a petition, a receiving order may be made and the normal bankruptcy proceedings follow. Although any creditor can also petition, the Director of Public Prosecutions is almost invariably the petitioner. Where the Director decides not to petition, he writes to each of the creditors explaining his decision, and creditors usually, having been influenced by the decision, forgo further action. In only a very few cases, however, have petitions for receiving orders been presented privately. In deciding whether to present a petition, the Director applies two criteria: first, whether the offender has sufficient assets to make bankruptcy proceedings worthwhile; and second, whether it is in the public interest to take proceedings in respect of those assets (so far as they can be ascertained at that stage) because, for example, such action might cause severe hardship to the criminal bankrupt's family. Once the decision has been taken to present a petition, most of the work after the receiving order has been made devolves upon the Official Receiver, although the Director's office is kept informed and continues to finance the proceedings.[11]

The real burden of criminal bankruptcy has fallen on the Insolvency Service, and no excessive administrative work has devolved on the Director of Public Prosecutions and his staff. Under the present law a criminal court can make a bankruptcy order only if it specifies the amount of the loss resulting from the offence, names the persons

---

9. Acts in respect of which the defendant had not been convicted are not 'other relevant . . . offences' within sect. 39(1)(b) and (2) and accordingly the amounts in them cannot be aggregated with those on which he has been convicted so as to supply the aggregated minimum: *Anderson v. DPP* [1978] A.C. 964.
10. Powers of Criminal Courts Act 1973, sect. 41 and Schedule 2.
11. ACPS report on *Sentences of Imprisonment – A review of maximum penalties*, chapter 15, p. 130, para 296.

appearing to have suffered that loss, and states the amount of that loss which it appears to the court that each of the persons has suffered.[12] The prosecution's inability to identify that particular loss and to relate it to a known victim reduces the scope or even applicability of criminal bankruptcy. In the case of major frauds, where it is impossible to prove the size of the fraud in concrete financial terms or to identify all the victims before a thorough investigation can be undertaken (which might take months or years), the scheme is inapplicable. In our view, criminal bankruptcy should be viewed in the same light as proceedings against delinquent directors of companies: as long as it is established that loss has been suffered equal to, or greater than the minimum limit, then all those who have suffered loss should be treated as creditors in the criminal bankruptcy, whether or not they are immediately identifiable and whether or not the amount in excess of the statutory minimum can be specifically ascertained.

In its report of 1978 the Advisory Council on the Penal System studied criminal bankruptcy orders made in England and Wales[13] up to the end of February 1978. This study[14] disclosed that the scheme had been limited in the scope of its application to the most serious cases, largely because considerations of cost and manpower had led prosecutors and courts to select only those cases where the recovery of substantial ill-gotten gains might assuage public anxiety, leaving it to the victim to seek elsewhere the recovery of the smaller amounts of money. In the wide discrepancy between the amount specified in the order and the known assets of the offender, the list reveals the inherent defect of applying criminal bankruptcy to large-scale fraud offenders on whom long-term imprisonment has been imposed. The key to the successful operation of criminal bankruptcy is the co-operation of the offender; where the offender is imprisoned for any length of time, co-operation has not so far been forthcoming. Thus in the short term the Insolvency Service has achieved few returns for victims, while there has been a significant addition to the existing workload of an overworked service. The lack of effective co-operation from offenders clearly has been a severe drawback to the scheme.

In the longer term there may be some real benefits from criminal

---

12. Powers of Criminal Courts Act 1973, sect. 39(3). No appeal lies against the making of a criminal bankruptcy order: sect. 40(1): *R v. Reilly* (1982) 75 Cr. App. R. 266.

13. Scotland has not introduced the measure, and the Dunpark Committee on Reparation by the Offender to the Victim in Scotland (Cmnd 6802, chapter 15) reported in 1977 that it felt unconvinced of the need or desire to confer upon the criminal courts the power to make criminal bankruptcy orders. The absence of a state bankruptcy service in Scotland is a powerful disincentive to any replication of the English provisions.

14. *Sentences of Imprisonment – A review of maximum penalties*, chapter 15 and Appendices, pp. 128–237 and 231–4 respectively.

bankruptcy which have yet to become discernible. A criminal bankruptcy order acts as a kind of permanent flypaper; it continues to apply after the offender has served his prison sentence, irrespective of his unco-operativeness during incarceration. Anything the discharged prisoner may purchase belongs to his trustee in bankruptcy. And under criminal bankruptcy any gifts or undervalued sales made on or after the earliest date on which the criminal offence has been committed can, on application to the Bankruptcy Court by the Official Receiver, be ordered to be transferred by any person acquiring the whole or part of the property given or sold at undervalue.[15] Furthermore, if powers were to be taken to deny the discharged prisoner the privilege of holding a passport, assets secreted abroad might become available to creditors.

The investigation of the criminal bankrupt's affairs depends almost exclusively on information provided by the bankrupt himself. The Insolvency Service has found that it has frequently proved slow, difficult and expensive to extract the necessary information. This is not to say that any scheme could be quick, easy or cheap. But unless there is the prospect of co-operation, the financial results will not justify the undue proportion of time the Insolvency Service is having to devote to criminal bankruptcy, and co-operation is unlikely from a prisoner serving a long term of imprisonment.[16] Normally, where a civil bankrupt fails to co-operate, the Official Receiver seeks an order of committal to prison, but this sanction is ineffective against the long-term prisoner. If committal proceedings were taken, the Bankruptcy Court would generally be bound to make an order which ran concurrently with the prison sentence, and it would in most cases be impractical to defer the institution of committal proceedings until the prisoner was released. To make any scheme effective it will have to be linked to a sentencing policy that envisaged a trade-off in return for collaboration with the enforcement agency.

The Advisory Council considered whether eligibility for parole might be used as an influence in improving co-operation. Whenever it is considering releasing a prisoner on parole the Parole Board is made aware of the existence of a criminal bankruptcy. The Advisory Council recommended that the Official Receiver should invariably be asked to indicate to the Parole Board at the moment of eligibility for parole (and at intervals thereafter) what state a prisoner's bankruptcy had

15. Powers of Criminal Courts Act 1973, para 10 of Sched 2. Surprisingly, no use of this provision appears to have been made to date.
16. The Bankruptcy Court does not rely exclusively on the bankrupt for information regarding his estate. The bankrupt's wife, mistress, business associates or professional advisers can, under the bankruptcy laws, be privately examined. *Sentences of Imprisonment.*

reached.[17] Such information is as likely as not to operate in the prisoner's favour. It would give the prisoner, moreover, a substantial opportunity to influence his own future by contributing to the successful execution of the order. Parole can have only a limited effect in solving this problem, since co-operation with the Insolvency Service could not be made an overriding criterion in the granting of parole. There will be cases where a prisoner co-operates but cannot be granted parole for other reasons. Nevertheless, there will be other cases where good co-operation will help to tip the scales in favour of an earlier release.

The criminal bankrupt can be charged with a bankruptcy offence if he fails to provide certain information. Sect. 154(1)(1) of the Bankruptcy Act 1914 already contains a provision making it a criminal offence punishable by imprisonment for up to two years if the bankrupt fails to disclose all his property and details about the disposal of any part of his property. The burden of proving that there was no intent to defraud is on the bankrupt. This offence does not, however, cover the failure to give information about his assets either by refusing to answer questions or by giving false information. There are good reasons for treating non-compliance with bankruptcy orders by a criminal bankrupt more strictly than that by his civil counterpart. If, in any case, a bankruptcy court were to make an order of committal for a fixed period in respect of non-compliance with its orders, such sentence would presumably have to be made to take effect consecutive to the current prison sentence (contrary to present practice) rather like a consecutive sentence of imprisonment in default of payment of a fine for another offence.

Throughout the discussions on the proposal for criminal bankruptcy and the ensuing legislative process, no attention was paid to dealing with two vital features of the experiment: namely, (i) that there could be no true investigation of the offender's financial situation either, in particular, before trial or, effectively, after the making of a criminal bankruptcy order; and (ii) that no link was contemplated between the results of bankruptcy administration and any reduction in sentence, either at the sentencing stage or by way of earlier release on parole licence. It was these two omissions from the experiment which decisively led the Cork Committee on Insolvency to recommend the re-examination of the existing criminal bankruptcy procedure.[18]

Given the avowedly limited and experimental nature of the scheme, criminal bankruptcy has been a disappointing failure. The Advisory

17. Sentences of Imprisonment, p. 132, para 299. footnote 2.
18. Para 1724(a), p. 387.

Council itself, in reviewing the first five years of the experiment in its report *Sentences of Imprisonment – a Review of Maximum Penalties*, concluded that in its short experimental phase criminal bankruptcy had not worked well, although the Council did hope that its proposals for change (if and when made through amending legislation) would render the sanction more fruitful.[19] So far no move has been made to implement these recommendations, although the Criminal Justice Act 1982 afforded a recent opportunity when changes were made to the courts' powers to make compensation orders.[20]

The Advisory Council did not argue for the abandonment of the existing scheme of criminal bankruptcy; it merely regretted its limited application as an additional sanction to imprisonment for the more serious fraud offenders. It perceived (as it had not done in its 1970 report) criminal bankruptcy as a penalty in its own right that could be deployed to claw back misappropriations by offenders, such that courts would be led more readily to sentence offenders to shorter terms of immediate imprisonment, or even impose either suspended sentences (whole or partial) or non-custodial penalties. In the context of a chronic crisis in the prison system because of persistent over-crowding, such use would provide welcome relief to a hard-pressed prison administration. But, no doubt because of the shortness of the experimental period, and the context in which the Advisory Council in 1978 was reviewing criminal bankruptcy, no radical re-think has been undertaken. Taken with the Cork Committee's distaste for any continuance of the experiment, equated as it is with civil bankruptcy which itself – if Cork is implemented – is to be replaced by a new code of insolvency, the time is ripe for a thorough re-appraisal in the context of enlarged powers of forfeiture.

Criminal bankruptcy was a brave attempt to inject into the criminal courts' range of sanctions a workable system of redress for crime. If it has misfired, in that it has been wholly unproductive in recovering for victims their losses suffered at the hands of criminals, there is still room for its retention, and even its extension. Our proposals for confiscation would not make the continuance of criminal bankruptcy either unnecessary or a duplication. Backed by essential pre-arrest, or at least pre-trial restraints, criminal bankruptcy could usefully take its place in the panoply of penal sanctions. If deployed to reduce the amount of, or even to negative the use of, imprisonment, it would be another useful tool to break the iron equation between crime and the penalty of imprisonment.

19. Para 311, p. 137.
20. See sect. 67, Criminal Justice Act 1982.

11 The assessment of means

In earlier chapters we noted that the powers of the criminal court to fine, and to make compensation orders were dependent on offenders' means. We have also suggested that, in some cases at least, forfeiture and confiscation orders should take account of the effect of the order on the defendant's financial position.

Where a monetary order is payable by instalments, the periodic sum is obviously of most immediate importance to offenders, but the courts have rightly said that their means must be considered as well in calculating the total amount payable.[1] A number of sentencers have ordered defendants to pay compensation which, in the instalments they could have afforded, would not have been completed for several years. The Court of Appeal has said that generally instalments of compensation orders should not extend more than two years[2] and, in the case of a fine not usually more than twelve months.[3]

The 'means' in question ought to be those of the defendant. Compensation orders and fines have been struck down where the income of a spouse,[4] a relative[5] or suspected partners in crime[6] were taken into account. This is in accordance with the Powers of Criminal Courts Act 1973.[7] It would also be wrong in principle if a defendant were to be punished for the other person's failure to make their expected contribution. The only exception to this rule is that parents may be ordered to pay compensation for loss or damage caused by their children.[8] Since the order is then made against the adults, it is clearly their income which is relevant. The general rule, though, raises difficulties similar to those considered in chapter 14. If by the time sentence is imposed compensation has been paid to the victim by a third party, should the sentencer reduce the penalty which would otherwise be appropriate? In chapter 14 we considered whether taking

1. *R v. Rizvi* (1979) 1 Cr. App. R(S) 307.
2. For example, *R v. Making* (1982) 4 Cr. App. R(S) 180.
3. For example *R v. Knight* (1981) 2 Cr. App. R(S) 82.
4. *R v. Baxter* [1974] Crim. L. R. 611CA.
5. *R v. Inwood* (1974) 60 Cr. App. R 70CA; *R v. Hunt, The Times*, 14 December 1982 C.A.
6. *R v. Po* [1974] Crim. L.R. 557.
7. 1973 Act, sect. 35(4): '. . . the court shall have regard to *his* means so far as they appear or are known to the court'.
8. Children and Young Persons Act 1933, sect. 55 (on conviction), and Children and Young Persons Act 1969, sect. 3(6) (in care proceedings), as amended by Criminal Justice Act 1982, sects. 26 and 27 respectively.

account of the defendant's own payment of compensation does not unduly favour wealthy defendants. If a reduction of the kind envisaged here is made, is there not a bias in favour of defendants with wealthy friends? In chapter 14 we suggest that inequality could there be avoided by assessing defendants' reparation against their financial ability to make compensation. A comparable task is more difficult in the present context because enquiries cannot so easily or properly be made about the ability of defendants' friends and relatives to make payments. On the other hand, of course, sentencers are understandably and rightly keen to see that, if possible, the victim of offences should receive compensation from whatever quarter, and there are undoubtedly cases where sentences are deferred to see if the promise of relatives or friends can be made good before the defendant is brought back to court.

The calculation of defendants' means is now made in a rough-and-ready and unsystematic way. In *R v. Wright*[9] the Court of Appeal said:

It is, of course a fundamental principle of sentencing that financial obligations must be matched to the ability to pay and there is an overriding consideration that financial obligations are to be subjected to this test but that does not mean that the Court has to set about on an inquisitorial function and dig out all the information that exists about an appellant's means. The appellant knows his means and is perfectly capable of putting them forward on his own initiative. If, as happened here, the Court is given rather meagre details of the appellant's means then it is the appellant's fault.

In *R v. Johnstone*[10] the Court said that it was no part of the prosecution's function to conduct a detailed enquiry of the defendant's means, and in *Lenihan v. West Yorkshire Metropolitan Police*[11] the Court warned against using the social enquiry report as a way of finding out whether the parents of a young offender ought to pay compensation.

Of course, defendants' means are a matter peculiarly within their own knowledge and there may be cases (though few) where defendants choose to understate their income. More commonly, in our experience, defendants will overstate their income and underplay their expenses. In some cases this may be in the belief that if a financial penalty appears to the Court to be feasible, it will not impose a sentence of imprisonment. The Court of Appeal has regularly said that this is not a proper approach (the Court ought first to consider whether a custodial sentence is necessary and, if it is not, it should not change its mind on learning that the defendant has no means to pay a

9. 12 November 1976 C.A. (unreported but see Sweet & Maxwell's *Current Sentencing Practice* JI.2(g)).
10. (1982) 4 Cr. App. R(S) 141.
11. (1981) 3 Cr. App. R(S) 42.

fine or other financial penalty), but the conventional wisdom persists.

In other cases, though, we think that defendants understate their expenses through ignorance of what properly can be taken into account. We know of no survey to test this hypothesis, but our own experience suggests it is often true. Where a defendant (as in *Wright*) is represented, it is obviously the lawyer's duty to obtain instructions as to the defendant's regular outgoings, but even among the profession, there seems to be no unanimity on whether, for instance, large but irregular items, such as children's clothing, should be allowed for. Consequently, while we agree that defendants should still be left to volunteer information about their means, a standard questionnaire or checklist should be composed and made available as a matter of course. This would be particularly helpful for unrepresented defendants.

Finally, we suggest that the periodic payments should match the intervals on which defendants receive their income. Defendants who receive supplementary or unemployment benefit fortnightly must often find it difficult to set aside and save the following week's instalment. If payment to the court had also to be made fortnightly, the incidence of default might diminish.

12 Third party interests

Each of the powers we are examining must acknowledge to differing degrees the rights of third parties in the property which is the potential subject of the court order.

(1) When third party interests should prevail

(a) Restitution

Where goods have been stolen from their owner or taken by a trick or by blackmail, the court sentencing the offender can order the property to be returned (see chapter 7). By then it may have been acquired by third parties. They will generally have no entitlement to retain the property because of the general principle that no one – including the offender – can give a better title than they have. The exceptions to this are many and notoriously complex. They were reviewed in 1966 by the Law Reform Committee,[1] but the Committee's report received only lukewarm support, and it was castigated by Professor Atiyah for not being based on adequate empirical research.[2] We felt that a thorough analysis of this area would have absorbed a disproportionate part of our committee's limited resources and was in any event not central to our main tasks. It is not then a topic which we have examined further or one on which we make any recommendations.

(b) Forfeiture

As chapter 8 explained, forfeiture powers can be intended either to take out of public circulation noxious substances whose very possession is an offence, or as a fine levied *in specie*. The attitude to third party interests should vary with each of these purposes. In the case of forbidden goods, such as dangerous drugs, it is understandable that the Court should be able to make a forfeiture order though the defendant was not their owner. In almost all cases, the true owner would also commit an offence by possessing them. This will not be invariably so, and we would wish the courts to have a discretion not to forfeit drugs on proof, for instance, that they were the property of a hospital or researcher who was licensed to possess them. Where

1. 1966 Cmnd 2958.
2. (1966) 29 M.L.R. 541.

possession of the forfeited goods is not *per se* an offence, or where the offence of possession depends on an intention which the owner may not share with the defendant, much greater respect ought to be accorded to the rights of third parties.

In general, we agree with the test in sect. 43(4)(b) of the Powers of Criminal Courts Act 1973 that third parties should be able to recover their property if they can show that they did not consent to the defendant having possession of the property or that they did not know, and had no reason to suspect that the property was likely to be used for the purpose which led the Court to contemplate a forfeiture order.

The Court may have to consider also the position of a third party who purchased the property from the defendant after its unlawful use. Such cases will be rare because sect. 43 can be invoked only where the defendant possessed or controlled the property at the time of his apprehension. The section gives no clear guidance as to how the Court would deal with this situation. An order under that section deprives the offender of 'his rights, if any' in the property. But if before sentence he has sold the article, he will have none. It is unlikely that Parliament intended the order to have retrospective effect; the deprivation of the rights of subsequent purchasers would have had to have been couched in much clearer language. We are not satisfied that as a matter of policy, subsequent purchasers ought to lose their rights even if they acquired the article in the knowledge that it had previously been involved in an unlawful enterprise. They would not thereby condone or assist the illegality. Nor (as in the case of subsequent acquisition of unlawful proceeds of an offence) is there a case for forfeiting the property in order to restore the *status quo*. Accordingly, we believe that sect. 43 of the 1973 Act should rightly be restricted to the forfeiture of the rights of the defendant and of those who, before the commission of the offence, knew or suspected that their property would be involved.

Where the revenue and customs authorities exercise their forfeiture powers (see chapter 6) third parties have no right to retain their property even if they proved their *bona fides*. They could only ask the Commissioners to exercise their statutory discretion to remit or mitigate the forfeiture. In many cases, the Commissioners have no doubt acceded to such requests, but in at least one reported case they did not.[3] The third party owners are now claiming that this forfeiture infringed their rights under the European Convention of Human Rights – Article 1 of the First Protocol. The European Commission

---

3. *Allgemeine Gold-und-Siblerscheideanstalt v. Commrs. of Customs and Excise* [1980] QB 390.

has declared the application admissible.[4] Whether the claim ultimately succeeds or not we think that the judiciary should judge the rights of third parties. We would like to see the courts have jurisdiction to order the return of seized property to third parties who, in the terms of sect. 43(4)(b) of the 1973 Act, could show that the property was either taken from them against their will or that they had no reason to suspect that it would be used for an unlawful purpose. If return was conditional on the exercise of all due care, the third party would still have an incentive to ensure that their goods were not used for a prohibited purpose. To deprive them of their goods, if this care had been taken, serves no useful purpose. It may lead indirectly to the real culprit paying more, as, for instance, when a hire company whose car has been forfeited obtains contractual damages against the hirer/smuggler, but in our view any additional penalty that is thought desirable and within the means of the perpetrator should be imposed directly. The indirect attack means that if the culprit does not have sufficient assets or income to pay fines or damages, the loss of the goods is borne by the innocent third party or their insurers. The Revenue can currently return goods on condition that a penalty is paid by the third party. If this is calculated according to the third party's complicity or negligence, the executive is effectively imposing a fine, for criminal conduct, a task which should be essentially a judicial one. In some cases it may be that the penalty is calculated according to the weight of the evidence against the third party. In our view a person against whom there is insufficient evidence ought to go unpunished, not receive a discounted sentence. In this case, a similar requirement of good faith *is* appropriate for subsequent purchasers. Otherwise they might benefit from buying untaxed goods more cheaply.

(c) Confiscation

Third party interests are clearly important here if specific property is confiscated. But similar issues may arise even if the Court imposes a pecuniary penalty calculated according to the profit which the defendant has made (as in the Australian system, see chapter 4). Although this obligation is purely personal and no question of third party

---

4. Application no. 9118/80. It was declared admissible on 9 March 1983. Article 1 of the First Protocol provides: 'Every natural or legal person is entitled to the peaceful enjoyment of his possessions except in the public interest and subject to the conditions provided for by law and by the general principles of international law.

    The preceding provision shall not, however, in any way impair the right of a state to enforce such laws as it deems necessary to control the use of property in accordance with the general interest or to secure payment of taxes or other contributions or penalties.' Cmnd 9221, 1952.

interests arises, similar issues may have to be considered if the defendant's property has been subjected to a pre-trial injunction and the Crown wishes the Court to order that the penalty be paid out of the frozen assets.

Broadly speaking, we believe that the right of the Crown to trace and confiscate the proceeds of an offence should be analogous to the right of civil plaintiffs to trace and seek restitution of their property. Consequently, if the property is acquired by a *bona fide* third party for value it should be irrecoverable. This test by itself leaves innocent donees vulnerable to confiscation. We think this is generally acceptable, but again, by analogy with the developing civil law of restitution, we would allow the Court to have a discretionary power to restore the goods to third party donees who had incurred expenditure or obligations in reliance on the gift.[5]

Our consultative document canvassed the possibility of the Court having a wider power to reach property in third party hands by analogy with its power to rescind transactions made shortly before a debtor becomes insolvent. This attracted no support and so, subject to what we have to say in chapter 10 on criminal bankruptcy we do not pursue it.

(2)   Standing, notice and appeal

It is axiomatic that third parties' interests can only be adequately protected if they have a right to be heard before they are deprived of their rights.

In some cases this means that the third party should have a right to be heard before any order is made. Some statutes already provide for this. Thus those claiming to be owners of allegedly obscene publications can appear and show causes why a forfeiture order should not be made.[6] The owners of property condemned by the Customs Commissioners have similar rights.

(a) Restitution

In our view, a like right should be given to a third party who wishes to oppose a restitution order under the Theft Act 1968. In *R v. Ferguson*[7] Lord Justice Salmon denied that any such right presently existed and gave this as one reason why courts should refuse to consider a restitution order if there 'was any doubt at all as to whether the goods belonged to a third party'. However in *Ferguson* the defendant had raised the issue of a third party's claim. In our view, third parties need

5. Goff and Jones, *The Law of Restitution*, 2nd edn. 1978, pp. 545–56.
6. Obscene Publications Act 1959, sect. 3.
7. *R v. Ferguson* [1970] 2 All ER 820.

their own *locus standi* in case the defendant is not so protective. It may be that on the third party's appearance the matter can be quickly resolved. If it cannot then, consistent with our attitude to compensation, restitution and confiscation, we would reluctantly agree that the present delays in criminal trials means that the Court should not attempt to resolve a complex dispute but should leave the victim, third party and defendant to litigate their differences in the civil courts.

(b) Forfeiture

Where a forfeiture order under sect. 43 of the Powers of Criminal Courts Act is made, there is not the same need for the third party to have standing before the criminal court. That court order only forfeits the defendant's interest in the property. Even if the order is made by the criminal court it is open to third parties to argue their innocence before the magistrates on an application under the Police (Property) Act 1897. On such an application, it is conceivable that they may wish to argue that their property was not within sect. 43(1) of the Act, i.e. that it was not used for the purposes of committing or facilitating the commission of an offence or was not intended by the defendant to be used for that purpose. Since a sect. 43 order should only be made in a clear case, it will be rare for such an argument to succeed, but it is possible that a defendant who did not own the property in question might not argue the matter with full vigour. Accordingly, we think that, with leave, the matter might be reopened on an application by the third party to recover their property. Evidence as to the property which was given at the trial should be admissible in such proceedings and the burden of proof on this issue should be on the third party.

Instead of bringing proceedings under the 1897 Act in a magistrates' court, third parties can bring a county court action against the police for conversion or wrongful interference with their goods. Although more expensive, this has two advantages. The action need only be commenced within six years, rather than the much shorter time limit of six months for challenging a sect. 43 order in the magistrates' courts.[8] Secondly, the claimants do not have to satisfy sect. 43(4)(b), i.e. they do not have to show that their property was taken involuntarily or that they were ignorant of its proposed unlawful use.

The overlapping jurisdiction of the county court is necessary to cater for the more complex disputes as to title which would be inappropriate for magistrates' courts. We can see also that a longer

8. See sect. 43(4)(a).

time limit is desirable, in part because the owner may not have been aware of the sect. 43 order (though we comment on this below) and in part because litigation in the county court does require more preparation and consultation. The police are not too hampered by the extra period within which an action can be brought, because they do have the power to sell the property after six months and, if the action is successful, they can then account for the proceeds.

(c) Confiscation

Before a confiscation order is made, third parties should again have standing to argue their *bona fides* before whichever tribunal determines whether their property is to be subject to the order or is to be used to satisfy it. A more difficult issue is whether third parties should be able to apply to free their property from a pre-trial freezing order. Our view is that they should, but only if the judge is persuaded that their application can be determined without prejudice to the defendant's pending criminal trial.

(3)   Notice

A right to be heard is only of use if third parties know that their property is in danger of forfeiture, confiscation or restitution. Some will know from their relationship with the defendant but others, particularly secured creditors (to whom we intend the term 'third party' to extend), might be ignorant of the possibility. In the United States, notice of civil forfeiture proceedings must be given personally to interested parties whose identities and addresses are known or easily obtainable. Missing or unknown persons can be given notice by an advertisement in a newspaper of a general circulation.[9] The English customs authorities are only required to notify anyone who to their knowledge is the owner of seized property.[10] An advertisement in an appropriate paper would not be an extravagant additional burden, particularly if it was subject to a minimum value of say, £1000.

Subject to a similar threshold, we think that the police should advertise orders under sect. 43, at least where possession of the property is not itself an offence.

(4)   Legal aid and appeal

In all the cases where we have referred to a right to be heard, it again would seem to follow that third parties without the necessary means should be able to obtain legal aid. Since, they are not themselves

9. *Mullane v. Central Hannover Bank & Trust Co.* 70 S.Ct. 652 (1950).
10. Customs and Excise Management Act 1979, Sched 3, para 1(a).

on trial, the civil legal aid system would be the more appropriate. Similarly, if a third party's submissions are rejected they ought also to be able to appeal.

13 Application of moneys or property received by the Courts

On sentencing an offender a court may decide that two or more of the penalties which we have discussed are appropriate. Stolen property may have been recovered; a victim of the offence may have been injured; a weapon or vehicle used in the commission of the crime may have been seized; and the proceeds of other illegal activity might have been traced. In addition the court may think that it should impose a fine. It may also order the defendant to pay all or part of the prosecution costs or to make a contribution towards his legal aid.

In chapter 14 we consider the appropriate relationship between these orders and whether for instance, a compensation order would justify a reduction in a fine. In this chapter we wish to assume that one or more of these monetary or proprietary penalties has been made and, on that assumption, to discuss the right use for property or moneys that are received, particularly where there is insufficient to satisfy all the orders. The obligation on the Court to consider the defendant's means before making a compensation order or imposing a fine should limit the circumstances where this conflict arises but, when it does, which should have priority?

(1) Money

Any money received from a convicted person is now used first to satisfy any compensation order.[1] Of course, for the defendant this has the collateral advantage that priority is given to discharging his or her civil liability to the victim. Some doubt as to the paramount position of compensation may also creep in where the real beneficiary of the order is an insurance company or some other concern with the ability to spread the loss. However, these are issues which we discussed in chapter 5 on the proper extent of the criminal court's power to make compensation orders. Once an order has been made, we agree that it ought to be given priority. This was also the unanimous view of those who sent representations to us.

---

1. Magistrates Courts Act 1980, sect. 139(a) for summary conviction (applied by sect. 41 Administration of Justice Act 1970 to orders made by the Crown Court).

Second preference is given to discharging any order as to the payment of prosecution costs.[2] Had these not been incurred none of the other orders would have been made.

The balance of any money received is credited to the defendant's fine. Fines are paid into the Consolidated Fund.[3] In chapter 5 we suggested that instead they should be used to subsidise a compensation fund for victims. We would suggest that money confiscated from an offender should also be used for the same purpose. To a limited extent profits of offences confiscated by way of fines may already be used for compensation. We imagine that it is relatively unusual for illegal transactions to cause loss for which compensation is necessary but where a defendant is convicted of several offences, some of which cause loss and some of which have yielded illegal profits, the fine in respect of the latter may be postponed to payment of compensation for the former.[4] Our proposal for a victim compensation fund is an extension of the same principle.

No specific rank or priority is given to legal aid contributions. They will be enforced by a magistrates' court.[5] In the absence of an express provision, the offender, like any other debtor, can presumably choose to appropriate his payment to this debt or to the other obligations imposed upon him by the court.

(2) Property

Some forms of property such as prohibited drugs or obscene publications are forfeited in order to take them out of circulation. No issue then arises as to their application. They ought to be destroyed.

Similarly, no question arises as to the use of property subject to a restitution order. An order may be refused because an owner knew of its intended use or because subsequent dealings with the property deprived him or her of title to it, but these are matters which we considered in chapter 12.

Issues do arise where property is forfeited (or subject to our recommended confiscation order) and there is no inherent objection to its

2. *Ibid.*, sect. 139(b).
3. Justices of the Peace Act 1979 sect. 61.
4. Though *quaere* whether Magistrates Court Act 1980 sect. 139 permits this since it sets priorities only for sums adjudged to be paid by a summary conviction. If each offence led to a separate conviction could a fine paid in respect of one be used to satisfy a compensation order in respect of another? We understand from the Home Office that when a defendant is convicted on more than one count at the same hearing it is the normal practice to treat this as one conviction and that payments are directed in accordance with sect. 139 of the 1980 Act. If for some reason the conviction on each count is recorded separately, it would be for the defendant when making payment to choose to which order it should be allocated.
5. Legal Aid Act 1974, sect. 35.

sale. What then should happen to the proceeds? The present position is confused. In the case of specific forfeiture powers, the proceeds are to be treated in the same way as a fine[6] and thus are apparently also to be paid into the Consolidated Fund.[7] Property forfeited under sect. 43 of the Powers of Criminal Courts Act 1973 is treated differently.[8] It comes under the regulations made under the Police (Property) Act 1879[9]. Under these, the costs of storage and disposal are a first charge. Secondly compensation may be paid to the person delivering the property to the police. Any balance is given to charity.[10] In neither case, it seems, can the proceeds be used to pay compensation to the victim of the offence. This conclusion is in line with recent decisions of the courts[11] holding that neither forfeiture nor restitution orders could be used as a form of security for the payment of compensation.

We think the position should be changed and the proceeds of forfeited or confiscated property should be available in the first place to compensate victims of the same offender and in the second place other victims through our proposed Victims' Compensation Fund. If this were accepted, a sentencing court might reasonably take account of the proceeds of such property in calculating the defendant's ability to pay compensation, though, if the property did not fetch its anticipated price, the Court should have the power to adjust its order accordingly.

6. Magistrates Court Act 1980 sect. 140.
7. We understand from the Home Office that this is the practice.
8. Powers of Criminal Courts Act 1973 sect. 43(4) & (5).
9. Police (Disposal of Property) Regulations 1975 S.I. 1975 no. 1474.
10. In practice some forces deduct little if any costs for storage. Although individual forces keep accounts, no central records are kept of how they dispose of their residual amounts or which charities are chosen.
11. *R v. Thibeault, The Times*, 23 April 1982; *R v. Kingston Upon Hull Justices ex parte Hartung* [1981] Crim. L.R. 42 [1981] RTR 262.

14 The relationship between orders to pay money or transfer property and other penalties

In this chapter we try to analyse the inter-relation between orders for compensation, confiscation, restitution and forfeiture and penalties of a more clearly punitive nature. Another closely related question is whether co-operation by an offender in paying compensation, returning stolen property or in computing, for the purpose of a confiscation order, the profitability of an offence ought to be rewarded by a reduction in other sentences. These two aspects merit separate consideration.

In *R v. Inwood*[1] Scarman L.J. said that 'compensation orders were not intended to enable offenders to buy themselves out of other penalties'. The powers of the Court to award compensation had been significantly broadened in the Criminal Justice Act 1972[2] since codified in the Powers of Criminal Courts Act 1973.[3] Two principles seem to lie behind this dictum. First, such a reward given to one defendant might seem to discriminate against another with no or fewer resources or prospects. Given an offender without the means to pay compensation, there would be no alternative but to impose the other penalty in full. Since that other penalty is frequently a prison sentence, imprisonment could then be seen as being explicitly a punishment for the poor. Second, compensation, restitution, forfeiture and confiscation orders discharge or reduce a defendant's civil liability or eliminate an advantage which he previously had over honest citizens. They try to restore the *status quo*; they do not punish. If co-operation is rewarded by reduced sentences, sentencing is turned into a market-place bargain and those with few resources suffer.

This attitude to compensation can be traced back to *R v. Lovett*.[4] A master whose servant was charged with theft told the Court that he

1. (1974) 60 Cr. App. R. 70 C.A.
2. Sect. 1; as to their earlier history see chapter 2.
3. Sect. 35.
4. (1870) 11 Cox's Criminal Cases 602.

would be happy with a compensation order (introduced that year by the Felony Act 1870). Sergeant Cox refused saying that this would be to support and condone a felony. He imposed what he described as a 'lenient' sentence of six months in prison. In *R v. West*[5], the Court of Appeal refused to adapt the common law power to adjourn a hearing to allow defendants an opportunity to pay back stolen money. The Lord Chief Justice thought it quite wrong 'to turn the criminal courts into a money-collecting agency'. Ten years later, in *R v. Collins*[6] a defendant was remanded on bail after conviction and before sentence to see if he would help with the recovery of stolen property. Again the Court of Appeal was critical. The trial judge should have decided immediately between prison and a probation order; it was undesirable to offer an implicit bargain.

However, another line of cases beginning in 1968, suggested a different attitude to 'implicit bargaining' in sentencing. In that year Dr Savundra was convicted of fraud. He was sentenced to eight years in prison and ordered to pay a fine of £50,000 or serve two years in default (there were a number of counts in the indictment and therefore the period in default could exceed the maximum of one year for a single count).

The Court of Appeal refused to disturb the fines saying:

The judge and this court cannot shut their eyes to the fact that when frauds are perpetrated on this scale it sometimes occurs that the criminal is conscious of the peril in which he stands of being prosecuted and takes the precaution of putting large sums of money out of the way of his creditors against the time he comes out of prison . . . £50,000 is a very small proportion of this man's plunder.[7]

It also upheld the sentence in default because a total of ten years would not have been unreasonable for offences of this kind.

This approach was followed in *R v. Harding*[8] and *R v. Lott-Carter*[9] where again the Court considered that the defendants would pay the fine out of the proceeds of the offence, and that, if they did not, the term of imprisonment plus the additional period in default was reasonable. In these cases the court was accepting that the defendants could 'buy themselves out of prison'. In a later case it has stressed that the keys to their cells must be in their own pockets. It was wrong for a

5. (1959) 43 Cr. App. R. 109.
6. (1969) 53 Crim. App. R. 385.
7. *R v. Savundranayagan and Walker* [1968] 1 WLR 1761, 1766.
8. 20 February 1974 unreported; but see Sweet & Maxwell, *Current Sentencing Practice* JI. 3(d).
9. (1978) 67 Cr. App. R. 404.

court to fine a carrier of heroin as well as sentence him to prison, in the expectation that other members of his organisation would pay the fine[10] (see also chapter 11). With this qualification, the courts moved the criminal law in the direction of revenue and customs law where the commissioners are given powers to compound offences before prosecutions are brought and to remit or mitigate penalties after they have been imposed (see chapter 6). The Commissioners' discretion is much wider, but the principle is comparable – the risk or length of imprisonment varies inversely with the degree of co-operation.

Another important aspect of this part of the criminal justice system is the power given to the Court to defer sentences for up to 6 months.[11] An express purpose of the new power is to allow the defendant an opportunity to make reparation. However, sentence can only be deferred with the defendant's consent. The previous Court of Appeal decisions (*West* and *Collins*) still, therefore, prevent a trial judge from adjourning a decision as to sentence under the common law powers in order to put pressure on an unwilling defendant to pay compensation or to give assistance in recovering property. Deferred sentences are also inappropriate where the circumstances would call for a substantial prison sentence even if the defendant responded positively. The Court of Appeal has said that if a favourable report is made at the end of the deferred period, a substantial custodial sentence would be wrong in principle.[12]

In the early part of our deliberations we were much concerned with the impact of the 1972 power of ordering compensation upon the sentencing practices of the courts. However, in the Criminal Justice Act 1982[13] Parliament has given the criminal courts a clear and explicit role as money-collecting agencies. To the expansion of the powers of ordering compensation and restitution given by previous legislation Parliament has added a further very significant power and a further almost equally significant duty. First it empowered judges to impose a compensation order as the sole penalty for the offence. In the strict logic of Scarman L.J.'s dictum this would mean that an order for compensation, however great, would be a less severe sentence than an absolute discharge. Second, courts are now required to give priority to compensation where an offender lacks the means to pay both compensation and a fine.

It is difficult to exaggerate the dramatic change this has made to the criminal justice system. It means that the sole response of a criminal

10. *R v. Po* [1974] Crim. L.R. 557.
11. Powers of Criminal Courts Act 1973, sect. 1(1).
12. *R v. Gilby* (1975) 61 Cr. App. R. 112.
13. Criminal Justice Act 1982, sect. 67.

court can, in appropriate cases, be the awarding of compensation. The belief that is articulated in chapter 1 that for many defendants the paying of compensation is a real burden and requires real sacrifice no doubt lies behind these important legislative changes. In practical terms a compensation order is a penalty. Similarly, a restitution order for an equivalent sum to the value of stolen goods may, if the goods have been sold and their proceeds dissipated, have a penal effect (see chapter 7).

Now that it is possible for a criminal court to do no more than make a compensation order it is inevitable that the ordering of compensation will be taken into account in deciding what other if any penalty is appropriate. Indeed, where a court decides that a monetary penalty is appropriate, it is required to reduce or extinguish the fine element in favour of compensation if the offender cannot pay both in full. No doubt guidance from the Court of Appeal as to whether and how far an award of compensation should affect the Court's decision as to other penalties will come in time. But as we have discussed the problems posed in detail it may not be inappropriate to express the views we have reached.

We believe that orders for the payment of money or transfer of property should be taken into account in calculating other sentences. Our approval of these orders has positive roots in our belief in the intrinsic value of redressing a wrong but it also has negative foundations. Prison is expensive, degrading and mainly harmful. In our view, particularly when, as in most property crimes, offenders do not present a danger of violence, it ought to be used much more rarely than it is.

However, there are obvious causes for concern as to the extent to which such orders should affect other penalties. These stem we think from two facts: first, the unique character of imprisonment as a punishment, and second, the fact that the affluence or poverty of offenders varies.

Imprisonment is not only the most unpleasant and feared punishment but also the punishment which is felt, rightly or wrongly, to be the only proper response to some offences and offenders. That response may be required for differing reasons. First, and in our view most justifiably, it may be needed in a few comparatively rare cases to protect society by segregating dangerous criminals away from it. Second, it may be felt necessary to imprison someone so as to announce to society that the offence for which he has been committed will not be tolerated. Third, it may be thought necessary to send someone to prison to deter him from offending again. Fourth, it may also be thought that, by sending people to prison, others will be deterred from like offending. Whatever we may think of these justifications for imprisonment, and considerable scepticism is felt by many as to the two latter ones, they are all part of current penological theory.

We have thought deeply as to whether and to what extent a proprietary order should be allowed to affect a sentence of imprisonment either by reducing it or by obliterating it altogether.

So far as a reason for imprisonment is the need to protect society from a dangerous offender by locking him away, we think it is obvious that no proprietary order could have any effect at all. In the other three cases the question posed is twofold: ought a proprietary order to take the place of imprisonment altogether and, the alternative question, ought a proprietary order to affect by reduction in length, a prison sentence?

These questions are we think of more theoretical than practical importance. Sentencing is not a precise exercise in logic. A sentencer has to consider in each case an offender and an offence. Offenders vary infinitely, offences not much less. Some offences will inevitably be met with a sentence of imprisonment whoever commits them. The reaction to others will depend on the offender. The response to a recidivist burglar will not be the same as to a teenage first offender. In the complicated equation which faces a sentencer it is inevitable that he will take into account any proprietary order he may make, and it is impossible to lay down hard and fast rules which will have universal application.

But practice is or ought to be founded on sound theory and to examine this question it is necessary to look more closely at the thought-processes of a judge or magistrate faced with the task of sentencing someone for a crime. And we are here only concerned with those cases where a prison sentence is, because of the nature of the offence or the character of the offender, a possible response. In such a case the thought-process of the sentencer is, or at least should be, this. In the case of this offence and offender is a sentence of imprisonment the only appropriate response of the criminal justice system? If yes, for what term? If for less than two years can I wholly suspend it? If no, can I suspend part of it? At each of these stages we think it would be unrealistic to think that a sentencer could be deterred from taking into account any proprietary order he was minded to make. The real problem is whether he should ever take it into account in deciding whether an immediate sentence of imprisonment should be imposed at all.

If a prison sentence is needed to announce to society that offences of that nature will not be tolerated, then not passing a sentence of imprisonment will have precisely the wrong effect: it will tell society that such offences are tolerated if money is paid. And if a prison sentence is felt to be necessary for deterrence then clearly any deterrent effect will be nil if as a result of the payment of compensation the offender avoids a prison sentence.

The theory then which should, in our opinion, underpin practice is that where a prison sentence is deemed necessary by the sentencer for one or more of these four reasons, then although a proprietary order, because it adds to an offender's burden, can properly be taken into account in reducing the length of a prison sentence, it ought not to take its place altogether.

However, we think that different conditions should, and inevitably will, apply in cases where an offender has, by his co-operation, assisted the Court in making a proprietary order. For a long time now the courts have been explicit that the fact that an offender has pleaded guilty is something which a court can and should take into account in sentencing. We think it justifiable to take an offender's co-operation into account in deciding whether and, if so, for how long a prison sentence should be imposed. Where, for instance, an offender has between the offence and trial made real efforts to save money to offer as compensation for his victim we think it would be wholly justifiable, in a borderline case, to allow such a demonstration of contrition to save him from imprisonment.

In cases where no question of imprisonment arises it seems to us that the offender's means and assets are of critical importance. If they are amply sufficient to pay compensation or restitution it is accurate to describe such orders as being merely a way of restoring the *status quo* and having no penal effect. Where defendants are not people of straw, civil proceedings are a real possibility and therefore the discharge of this civil liability by the payment of compensation or restitution is of more than theoretical importance.

By focusing on the defendant's ability to pay compensation or restitution, the Court may also allay fears that rich defendants are at an advantage. Our concern with equity between defendants is not confined to different treatment of co-accused. The contrast is less stark but no less unfair if the two differently treated defendants appeared in different cases and before different courts. In the experience of some of the members of our committee, courts do distinguish between defendants well able to pay compensation and those who cannot. Even small contributions by the latter, if they have involved extra effort or sacrifice, will be used to justify lighter penalties of other kinds. If even this is impossible, compensation in kind through community service ought to be considered.

Our committee approved of taking compensation, restitution and confiscation orders into account in calculating other sentences but short of allowing offenders to avoid prison sentences which seem called for by one of the considerations we have listed. We would go further and encourage the courts to do so and to make more use of fines where the means or assets of the defendant are such that the other orders will not have a penal effect. We disagree with the principle that fines should not be increased in the case of wealthy defendants.[14] If the offence is one where imprisonment is not appropriate (see above), but the defendant is sufficiently wealthy that the normal scale fine would leave little impression, we can see no reason why the Court should not tailor its financial penalty to the circumstances of the defendant. The Scandinavian system of 'day fines', where a fine is calculated as a multiple of the amount the defendant earns in a day, deserves a trial project in this country.

14. For example, *R v. Markwick* (1953) 37 Cr. App. R. 125.

15 International aspects

The Operation Julie case illustrated the relative ease with which illegal proceeds can be transferred out of the country. The profits of the drug sales were converted into French real estate, krugerrands and gold bars deposited in Swiss bank accounts. This international aspect of the recovery of the unlawful gains causes problems of investigation, jurisdiction and the enforcement of court orders. A system of confiscation which cannot reach beyond national boundaries will only catch the stupid, the slow, the small-timers, and those who are inextricably bound to the domestic economy either because their illegality is a marginal side of a lawful enterprise or by their investment of illegal proceeds. Nonetheless, because national sovereignty is such a delicate issue solutions will ultimately depend on diplomacy.

A measure of international co-operation has been achieved in the taking of evidence for foreign criminal proceedings. By the Evidence (Proceedings in Other Jurisdictions) Act 1975 sect. 5, English courts can order the examination of witness and the production of specified documents for use in foreign criminal proceedings. A prosecution must be under way and not be of a political character. Witnesses are accorded the normal privileges against self-incrimination (sect. 3). These powers are narrower than the assistance English courts will give in assembling evidence for foreign civil proceedings. Then, they may, for instance, order the preservation of property pending a decision: this cannot be done for foreign criminal proceedings.[1]

Although English courts are thus prepared to assist in the taking of evidence for foreign prosecutions they are extremely reluctant to admit foreign depositions in English criminal proceedings. This is understandable when the question is one of guilt, given the role of the jury and the importance we place on oral evidence with its opportunity to study a witness's expressions and demeanour. However, on an issue which might arise after conviction in relation to monetary or proprietary penalties there ought to be a greater willingness to admit evidence taken abroad.

The 1975 Act relates to the taking of evidence once a prosecution

---

1. Civil Jurisdiction and Judgments Act 1982, sect. 25. The power applies to litigation in any country which is a party to the EEC Convention on Jurisdiction and Enforcement of Judgments 1968 but it may be extended by Order-in-Council-to other countries.

has started. There is much less co-operation at the earlier stage of gathering evidence and following leads. The Interpol network provides a forum for exchange of information of a general kind. Our Committee benefited from this and we received via Interpol copies of legislation relating to forfeiture and confiscation in other jurisdictions. The network is used in individual cases and some assistance is given in the tracing of stolen property and illegal gains, but it is powerless to overcome the major obstacles to tracing such property, notably bank secrecy laws. Indeed British police making enquiries in countries such as Switzerland have occasionally been arrested for suspected violation of their laws of confidence. It is no easy matter to negotiate an exception to bank secrecy laws for criminal investigation. Many small states have attracted investors by the twin charms of low taxation and unyielding maintenance of commercial secrecy. It has taken the diplomatic might of the United States decades to reach a bilateral agreement with Switzerland for limited access to bank records for the purpose of tracing laundered money.

The UK is not a party to the European Convention on Mutual Assistance in Criminal Matters,[2] but it has subscribed to the Single Convention on Narcotic Drugs 1961.[3] Consequently it is an offence, triable in the UK, to assist in or to induce a breach of the laws which correspond to the Misuse of Drugs Act 1971 in other state parties to the Convention.[4] Further, magistrates have power to issue search warrants for documents in the UK relating to or connected with transactions which have or would infringe such laws.[5] As this example suggests, international co-operation to any significant degree is more likely to be limited to particular crimes.

Detecting movement of 'dirty money' out of the United Kingdom has become much more difficult since the abolition of exchange control. By comparison even quite small currency dealings are monitored in the United States. Under the Federal Bank Secrecy Act of 1970 individuals must report movements over $5000. They must also report any foreign bank accounts. Currency exchanges over $10,000 must be notified by banks. There are the predictable problems of delayed and inadequate compliance and the shortage of staff to analyse the information, but a small study by the Comptroller-General's report in 1981 showed that of thirty-one cases where forfeiture or confiscation of drug proceeds were involved, four had made use of currency or bank reports.[6]

2. 1959 European Treaty Series 30.
3. Cmnd 1580.
4. Misuse of Drugs Act 1971, sects. 20, 36.
5. *Ibid.*, sect. 23.
6. 'Asset-Forfeiture: A Seldom Used Tool in Combatting Drug Trafficking', Comptroller-General of United States, (1981).

Even where an investigation is successful and illegal proceeds are traced to foreign-held assets, the English courts are limited in their powers to make orders in respect of them. They have no jurisdiction over and cannot confiscate foreign land such as the French chateaux owned by the Operation Julie defendants. The Court does have jurisdiction in relation to personal property but foreign courts would still refuse to recognise that the order had transferred title or property rights to the crown unless the state had taken actual possession before the goods were moved abroad.[8] These principles were raised in 1983 in a claim by the New Zealand government to recover an antique Maori object which had been illegally exported from New Zealand and had thereby become subject to forfeiture to the New Zealand government. The House of Lords held that on the construction of the New Zealand legislation, the statue had not actually been forfeit but was only liable to forfeiture.[9] The Court of Appeal had held (*obiter*) that in any event the New Zealand government was seeking the assistance of the English courts to enforce a penal law.[10]

A compensation order is regarded differently. Although made by one state, criminal courts in others will generally recognise and enforce it.[11] We imagine that a restitution order would be similarly treated. In practice we doubt whether this is of great significance. Few victims are likely to have the funds to pursue foreign litigation against a defendant who has been convicted of a criminal offence.

An alternative, though second best, way of reaching assets held abroad would be for the Court to make a personal order for the payment of compensation or a pecuniary penalty by way of confiscation on the basis that this can be paid out of the foreign assets. The threat of a sentence of imprisonment in default may induce some to repatriate their funds. The Court of Appeal justified in this way the substantial fine which had been imposed on Dr Savundra at the same time as a prison sentence.[12] Similarly, in *R v. Hill*[13] the Court agreed that a fine could be combined with a criminal bankruptcy order where there was credible evidence that the defendant had substantial foreign holdings.

A complication of a different kind can occur where there are competing claims to the illegal proceeds. In the Operation Julie case, the law of the Swiss canton, where some of the proceeds were located,

7. *R v. Cuthbertson* [1980] 2 All ER 401, 406
8. *Brokaw v. Seatrain U.K. Ltd* [1971] 2 Q.B. 476.
9. *A-G for New Zealand v. Ortiz* [1983] 2 All ER 93 H.L.
10. *Ibid.* [1982] 3 All ER 432 C.A.
11. *Raulin v. Fischer* [1911] 2 K.B. 93; cf. Civil Judgments and Jurisdiction Act 1982 Sched. 1, Art. 5(4).
12. *R v. Savundranayagan and Walker* [1968] 1 WLR 1761.
13. [1983] Crim. L.R. 119.

forfeited to the canton government property obtained as a result of an offence under Swiss *or foreign laws*. Canada has a similar provision.[14] This complication may be thought to be of less importance: the moral basis for confiscation is that defendants ought not to profit from their wrongs. The benefit to the state is of secondary importance. Others may feel that this order of priorities assumes an altruism which rarely permeates the cynicism of international relations. Perhaps, if confiscation becomes a more popular way of punishing profitable crimes, there will be interstate disputes reminiscent of the medieval barons' jealousy of Plantagenet kings for turning felonies into treason and so depriving them of their profitable escheats.

---

14. Criminal Code sect. 312.
   'Everyone commits an offence who has in his possession any property or thing or any proceeds of any property or thing knowing that all or any part of it was obtained by or derived directly or indirectly from
   (a) the commission in Canada of an offence punishable by indictment; or
   (b) an act or omission anywhere that, if it had occurred in Canada would have consituted an offence punishable by indictment.'
   By creating an *offence* of possession of property or proceeds derived from another offence, sect. 312 follows the model of the Racketeering Statute (RICO) in the U.S. See chapter 4.

Note of Dissent
by Andrew Nicol and Clive Soley

(1) 'Sample counts'

The chapters on Confiscation and Compensation propose that defendants may be ordered to pay compensation or be deprived of profits by a confiscation order in relation to offences with which they have not been charged, of which they have not been convicted and which they have not admitted. It is said that this would be appropriate where the defendant has been convicted of other counts which the prosecution has submitted are representative of a continuing course of wrongdoing and that a finding of guilty on the sample charges justifies ordering compensation or confiscation for the whole period. In our view it does not. It is contrary to a basic principle of our criminal justice system to sentence a person for an offence that has not been proved or admitted.

The other members of the Committee would empower the judge to resolve a disputed issue of whether the defendant were guilty of further wrongdoing. This is not satisfactory in our view. Defendants are entitled to have allegations of serious criminality resolved not by a judge but by a jury and we fail to see why they should lose this right because they have been convicted of other, different offences.

The proposal is made apparently so as to save court time. Yet we do not see how this can be done without depriving the defendant of proper procedural safeguards. The other members of the Committee suggest that the defendant should be asked the basis of his denial of the other offences. It is a novel departure in our criminal procedure to ask the defendant to explain his plea of 'not guilty'. It would also be contrary to the European Convention on Human Rights, Article 6(2) of which provides that 'everyone charged with a criminal offence shall be presumed innocent until proved guilty according to law'. It ought not to be the *defendant* who has to explain his or her denial but the prosecution who must prove its case.

The other members of the Committee envisage that the prosecution might be content to rely only on evidence presented on the charged offences. If this is so, it is hard to see how the 'sample count' procedure will have saved any court time. It may be, of course, that the defendant would have pursued lines of cross-examination in relation to the uncharged offences that were not relevant or were otherwise inadmissible on the charged counts. What are to be his or her rights after conviction? May he or she insist on the witnesses being recalled? If so, again it is questionable whether the sample count procedure will save any time. Similarly, if the uncharged offences can only be proved by calling further evidence, it is difficult to see what economies are to be made except that since the judge is the tribunal of fact, it will be unnecessary to sum up the evidence, and the pace of the proceedings may be slightly faster. These savings are marginal and are achieved only at the cost of depriving the defendant of what we regard as the important right of trial by jury.

The other members argue that the judge is not concerned with questions of criminal liability but with whether in respect of the uncharged offences a claim for compensation or confiscation has been made out. We do not accept this distinction. Confiscation, as we have defined it, is 'depriving the offender of the proceeds or the profits of crime'. This quite clearly ought to be dependent on a crime having been committed and the defendant having committed it and thereby earned the profits in question. A better case could be made for saying that compensation is not punishment, but this is the premise of Lord Scarman's *dictum* in *R v. Inwood* that compensation should not affect other sentences. Yet the Committee as a whole does not share Lord Scarman's view (see chapter 4). It does believe that compensation should be taken into account in fixing other penalties. It approves of the change introduced by the Criminal Justice Act 1982 to allow compensation to be the only sentence imposed. The fact that defendants who fail to fulfil compensation orders may be sent to prison whereas civil debtors cannot is a further indication that compensation orders are a form of punishment. One purpose of compensation and confiscation is to restore the *status quo ante*, but when imposed by a criminal court they are also forms of punishment. As Jeremy Bentham said in the quotation cited in chapter 1, 'Compensation will answer the purpose of punishment.'

The other members of the Committee appear to recognise this when they propose that legislation make clear that the service of a 'sample count' notice should preclude future prosecution for any of the uncharged offences included in the notice. In the absence of such a provision, the uncharged offences that were included in the calculation of compensation or confiscation would not count as convictions and would not give the defendant a defence of *autrefois convict* if a later prosecution were initiated. The other members of the Committee rightly recognise that this would be unjust. It would be unjust because the defendant would then be subjected to double punishment: the first would be regarded as nonetheless punishment because it took the form of a compensation or confiscation order.

We read the House of Lords decision in *DPP v. Anderson* more widely than the Court of Appeal did in *R v. Price*. While the Law Lords were immediately concerned with a criminal bankruptcy order Lord Diplock's review of the sample count procedure and his insistence that the defendant's consent was a necessary condition to uncharged offences forming the basis of a sentence was couched in general terms. The Court of Appeal approved in *R v. Price* of the trial judge basing his sentence on 'the reality of the situation', a phrase which the other members of the Committee invoke. But the phrase advances the argument no further: it only begs the question 'What reality?' Our response would be that the sentence should be confined to the reality of the jury's verdict or the defendant's admissions in asking for other offences to be taken into consideration. Thus, whatever the true view of the authorities, we endorse the opinion of D.A. Thomas (see above p. 79) that it is wrong in principle to base a sentence on uncharged, unadmitted offences.

It follows that in the hypothetical extension of *Anderson's* case which the other members postulate we think the judge would be wrong to aim at relieving the defendants of the 'ill-gotten gains' of the uncharged offences. Because the other members hypothesise that Anderson was guilty of all twenty offences this may seem an unfair result, but Anderson did not agree that he was guilty of these offences; he did not agree that they should be taken into consideration in calculating his sentence. Whatever a defendant's hypothetical or real guilt, it seems axiomatic to us and a corollary of the presumption of innocence that he can put the prosecution to their proof. Further the proper tribunal to decide whether their case is made out is the jury.

Our view need not lead to overloading of indictments or the prolonging of trials. The other members of the Committee quote Lord Salmon's stricture as to the practice of doing this. However Lord Salmon was in complete agreement with Lord Diplock and prefaced his observation by saying that 'nothing in [Lord Diplock's] speech would justify increasing the number of counts included in the indictment' ([1978] 2 All ER at p. 516). We share this view. A long trial does not incline a jury towards either side and further counts may cause such confusion that unmeritorious acquittals result. This, in addition to the waste of public time and money of which Lord Salmon spoke, ought to dissuade prosecutors from overloading indictments.

(2)   The 'clear case' requirement

The other members of the Committee regard the 'clear case' requirement as a necessary expedient given the long delays in bringing criminal cases to trial but regard the limitation as wrong in principle. We think it right in principle.

The criminal process does not have the preliminary stages which in civil litigation vitally assist the parties. A plaintiff in civil proceedings must particularise his or her claim. If insufficient details are given for the defendant to know what it is that the plaintiff is asserting further and better particulars can be demanded. Likewise the defendant must make clear which allegations are accepted and which denied. Both sides must make 'discovery', that is disclose to each other all the relevant documents in their possession whether they assist or hurt their case. The Court can insist, if necessary, that the litigant make further discovery, if the first is not complete. These procedures are vital not only for questions of liability but also for questions of the amount of any damages which the plaintiff is due ('quantum'). It is not uncommon for quantum to be as contentious as liability. An offence may, for instance, be alleged to have caused economic loss, such as lost business or lost commercial opportunities. Proving such loss, though, may require complex adjustments to be made between one accounting period and another or difficult issues as to whether the loss really was due to the offence or some other cause. Consequently, we do not accept that the resolution of the issue of criminal liability (on whatever standard of proof) renders unnecessary as to these issues the procedures for particularising the claims in relation to quantum or discovery of documents on these issues. As long as the criminal courts are limited to 'clear cases' this may not matter (though even here we agree with other members that victims ought to produce receipts of bills or other documents which they rely upon), but it is the 'unclear cases' where these procedures are likely to be most unimportant.

The other members' proposal does include a scheme for particularising loss and making discovery. This is important. The details may be apparent from the prosecution's statements, but then again they may not. The statements will involve evidence of whether the crime was committed. That may or may not include evidence of the extent of any loss caused by the crime. In magistrates' courts, of course, defendants are not generally given even this information in advance. Even where prosecution statements are disclosed, they tell the defendant the evidence at the prosecutor's disposal, they do not particularise the allegations of loss for which the prosecutor will seek compensation. Civil procedure has for a long time distinguished between the distinct functions of pleadings, which state a party's case succinctly and evidence which is used to prove those allegations. Both are necessary. However, to bring the procedure proposed by the other members of the Committee into line with civil proceedings it would be necessary to allow the defendant to argue that the particulars were insufficient and that further and better details should be given or to require the victim to make further discovery or to swear an affidavit that that already made was complete. These procedures would in our view be necessary to protect the defendant, and yet they sit uneasily in a criminal process.

By definition we are concerned only with complex issues of quantum. These can arise in small as well as large claims. We are not therefore persuaded that the statutory limitation on the power of magistrates to award compensation will largely ensure that they do not have to consider such complexities. Consequently, we do see the 'clear case' requirement as being necessary to ensure that relatively inexperienced magistrates are not asked to resolve such issues. It may be thought that no similar concern is necessary in relation to the crown court where judges may, in theory, sit also as county court judges. In practice judges (at least in some areas) are required to specialise to a degree that their work keeps them exclusively in one field or the other. If complex cases of compensation were transferred to a nominated judge with civil judicial experience, then part of our objection might be taken care of. However, the complexity of issues of compensation may arise in serious or trivial offences and in those which involve greater or lesser problems on the issue of criminal liability. We doubt whether any foreseeable allocation of resources to the criminal justice system would permit courts' administrators the flexibility which the other members' proposal would require.

The 'clear case' principle can also save the Court having to resolve complex issues of the exact amount of the victim's loss. We quite agree that the Court should be able to order compensation for the core or clearly proveable part of the loss even though its full extent is a matter of complex dispute. The victim, if he or she wishes, can pursue a civil claim for an additional sum.

Finally, we do not agree that in the long run the majority's proposal would not place a further burden on the courts. Compensation proceedings in the criminal process will inevitably involve court time and for 'unclear cases' considerable time. Civil proceedings by the victim, if they follow the pattern of the vast majority of civil cases, will settle before they get to to court. Further, once defendants know that they are at risk of being ordered to pay compensation for complex civil liability, they may be less willing to plead guilty. As we observed in chapter 3, criminal convictions rank only as *prima facie* evidence in civil proceedings and may be rebutted by contrary evidence in part because it was recognised that some defendants choose not to advance a defence which they may have if the likely punishment for a guilty plea was only a small fine. Consequently we see the abolition of the clear case requirement leading to greater work for the criminal courts (in hearing more contested pleas and in resolving these complex issues) and we very much doubt that this will be matched by a saving in civil court time.

In our view the 'clear case' requirement is defensible, both for the practical reasons which the other members give and, for the reasons we give above, in principle.

Recommendations

A. Compensation

1. There should be a power to vary or extinguish a compensation order in the light of changes in the defendant's financial circumstances. (p. 53).

2. Dependants of a deceased victim should be eligible for compensation (p. 53).

3. Guidelines as to the current level of compensation for personal injuries in the civil system should be provided to criminal courts by the Criminal Injuries Compensation Board. These guidelines should be reviewed periodically (p. 56).

4. The restriction on the power to order compensation to clear cases must be retained while there continues to be such a backlong of cases waiting to be heard in the criminal courts. This restriction is not justified in principle but is at the present time acceptable in practice.*
(p. 57).

5. As in a civil suit, receipts, estimates and reports relating to loss for which compensation will be claimed in the event of a conviction should be disclosed to the defendant in good time before the trial. (p. 59).

6. Sentencers should be under a duty to consider whether compensation is appropriate, but no order should be made if the victim waives his right to compensation. (p. 61).

7. A pilot scheme should test the feasibility of providing more financial assistance for victims by a Victim Compensation Fund. It would be funded by the proceeds of the proposed new confiscation orders, together with fines and the proceeds of sale of forfeited property. On the assumption that there are available resources the Fund might make payments
   (a) to all victims;
   or (b) to victims where the offender was convicted and ordered to pay compensation by instalments. The victim would benefit from a lump sum payment immediately the order was made. The instalments would reimburse the fund;
   or (c) to uninsured victims who would otherwise suffer hardship by

* See dissenting note of two members.

the offence. The objective in this case would be compensation for personal injury below the Criminal Injuries Compensation Scheme's present limit of £400 and for small property losses.* (p. 64).

8. Cautions in lieu of prosecution should be dependant on the offender signing an admission of guilt. A copy of this should be given to the victim (if any) of the offence. The victim should be able to apply to a magistrates' court for a compensation or restitution order and the application should be considered in the same way as if the defendant had been convicted. The admission should be admissible evidence in a civil suit by the victim in the same way that a conviction now is. (p. 68).

B. Confiscation

9. Criminal courts should have the power to order the confiscation of proceeds of an offence of which the defendant has been convicted or asked to be taken into consideration. There should be a prescribed minimum amount below which no confiscation order could be made, but once that limit is established there should be no maximum limit. (p. 74).

10. Only crown courts should have the power to make confiscation orders, but magistrates should be able to commit defendants to the crown court with a view to a confiscation order being made. Committal for this sole purpose should be possible even though the offence is only triable summarily. Crown Courts should be required to consider whether a confiscation order should be made and Magistrates' Courts to consider whether to commit for consideration of the making of a confiscation order. (p. 74).

11. The Crown should give a defendant notice in advance of trial if a confiscation order will be sought. (p. 74).

12. The object of a confiscation order would be to restore the *status quo ante* the offence and, therefore, to reach only the net profit made by the defendant. Only expenses actually paid would, however be deductable, and consideration should be given to requiring the defendant to identify the payee. (p. 74).

13. The burden of proving the amount of the gross receipts should be on the Crown, but evidence of the street value of illegal commodities should be admissible. The defendant should have the burden of proving any allowable expenses. (p. 75).

14. The calculation of the proceeds should be made by the trial judge, but where the process is likely to be too time-consuming, he should be free to direct an account to be taken by another judicial official

---

* One member dissents.

(analogously to the civil procedure for calculating an account of profits). Sentence should be deferred pending such an enquiry, except that if an immediate sentence of imprisonment is appropriate it should be imposed at once. At the resumed hearing, the judge might take account of the defendant's co-operation or lack of co-operation, but not by imposing or lengthening an immediate prison sentence. (p. 81).

15. Where a defendant is charged with and convicted of sample counts, a compensation or confiscation order may relate to the whole course of dealing. This should be dependent upon the prosecution giving the defendant notice in advance of trial that the charged counts are regarded as samples, and of their intention to seek an order in relation to a specified period of illegal dealing. The notice should include any evidence which would be inadmissible on the charged counts. Service of a notice would preclude future prosecution for any offence covered by the notice. On conviction of the charged offences, any dispute as to the extent of the defendant's liability to pay compensation or confiscation should be resolved by the trial judge.* (p. 79).

16. A defendant convicted of wholesale supply of Class A or B drugs to a street value of £100,000 or more should have the burden of proving that assets acquired after the date of the first proved offence were legitimately obtained. Property not shown to be lawfully obtained might be made the subject of confiscation orders and illegal profits might be traced into the hands of family and friends. However the defendant should be immune from prosecution in relation to any offences disclosed by him on such an enquiry.* (p. 82).

C. Restitution

17. The Theft Act 1968 sect. 28(4), which allows the court to make a restitution order only if sufficient evidence was given at the trial or if the defendant has made admissions, should be repealed as unnecessary. (p. 87).

18. As in the civil system, a court should have power to attach conditions to a restitution order to see that the victim is not left better off than if the offence had not been committed. (p. 87).

19. The Theft Act 1968 sect. 28(1)(c), which gives the Court the power to order a thief to pay compensation to the deprived owner, should be repealed as unnecessary. The general power to order compensation under the Powers of Criminal Courts Act 1973 sect. 35 adequately covers all situations where compensation is appropriate. (p. 90).

---

* See dissenting note of two members.

20. Where a thief has property which was acquired with the proceeds of thefts from a number of victims, the Courts should be able to order the sale of that property and compensate the victims *pro rata*. (p. 91).

21. A court should be able to make a restitution order of the proceeds of stolen goods (under sect. 28(1)(b) of the Theft Act 1968) whether or not an application is made by the victim. This would make the procedure consistent with its other powers under sect. 28 and its powers to make a compensation order. (p. 92).

22. The procedure under the Police (Property) Act 1897 for determining how to dispose of property in the possession of the police should continue to be initiated by an application or complaint. However in either case the magistrates' court which hears the application should be able to award costs. If the police act as interpleaders and play a purely passive role in the application they ought not to be liable for costs. If they oppose the application for the return of the property to assist the Court to test the validity of the application, but the application ultimately succeeds, the magistrates' court should be able to order the payment of costs out of central funds. (p. 93).

D. Forfeiture

23. Although sect. 43 of the Powers of Criminal Courts Act 1973 confers a broad power of forfeiture, it is sensible to retain powers in other statutes so far as they relate to specific articles of property whose possession is prohibited. To the extent that specific powers cause them to overlap with sect. 43 they should be amended to replicate the general power. (p. 95).

24. In rare cases it is necessary to have a procedure for seizing and forfeiting property though its owner has not been convicted of an offence. The legality of such forfeitures can now usually be tested in condemnation of forfeiture proceedings. Owners of such property should however always have the right to insist that they stand trial before suffering the loss of their goods. (p. 95).

25. Apart from the cases referred to in 24 above, forfeiture should relate only to offences of which the defendant was convicted or asked to be taken into consideration. (p. 98).

26. Where the purpose of forfeiture is as a cumulative penalty (for instance when a getaway car is forfeited), and not to take dangerous or prohibited goods out of circulation, consideration should be given to allowing the defendant to pay a pecuniary penalty commensurate with the value of the goods and in effect to buy them back. (p. 99).

27. The broad power of forfeiture in sect. 43 of the Powers of Criminal Courts Act 1973 should extend to any property of the defendant's which has been lawfully seized at any time by the police

or other authorities. This should replace the present requirement that only property in the possession or control of the defendant at the time of his arrest can be forfeited. (p. 100).

28. The power in sect. 43 should no longer be limited to offences which are punishable on indictment with two years' imprisonment or more. Instead a court should have powr to make a forfeiture order if the value of the property does not exceed the maximum fine for the offence. If the defendant is also fined or ordered to pay compensation, the total of the financial penalties (including the value of any forfeited property) should not exceed the maximum fine for the offence. (p. 101).

E. Pre-trial restraint

29. On the application of the police or prosecuting authority a high court judge should have the power to grant, on appropriate terms, an order freezing specific assets or the defendant's assets generally, if there is a *prima facie* case that he has committed an indictable offence and it appears to the Court likely that on conviction the Court of trial would impose a fine and or a compensation order totalling £10,000 or more. (p. 108).

30. The order would initially be made *ex parte*, but the defendant should be at liberty at any time to apply to have the order discharged or varied, in particular so that he can realise assets for living expenses or the cost of his defence. (p. 108).

31. If the defendant is later acquitted, the trial judge should have a discretion (as he currently has in relation to the defendant's legal costs) to order the payment of compensation in a stated amount or order an enquiry as to damages. (p. 109).

32. On the application of a victim who wishes to pursue a civil claim, procedures should be established for continuing the injunction. (p. 109).

33. Once an order freezing the defendant's assets has been obtained by the police or prosecution they should have wider powers to demand information from third parties who are thought to hold those assets. There is a good deal to be said against any general power to order the defendant to disclose where his assets are to make discovery relating to them. (p. 109).

34. A receiver should be appointed under the Director of Public Prosecutions to supervise property held under freezing orders. (p. 110).

35. The police should *not* be granted powers to search defendants' premises specifically for evidence of assets. (p. 111).

---

* See note of dissent by two members

F. Criminal bankruptcy

36. Although criminal bankruptcy has been largely unproductive, it should be retained with modifications in the light of these recommendations. Together with the other measures proposed it can play a useful part in the array of sanctions available to the court. Co-operation by the imprisoned offender with the Official Receiver should be a factor in considering early release on parole licence. (p. 118).

37. So far as criminal bankruptcy becomes a successful method of re-recovering the proceeds of crime it should encourage sentencers either to avoid immediate sentences of imprisonment or to reduce such sentences. (p. 119).

G. Assessment of means

38. A standard questionnaire should be prepared to elicit fuller information about a defendant's means. (p. 122).

39. Periodic payments of fines, compensation orders, etc. should wherever possible match the intervals at which the defendant receives his income. (p. 122).

H. Third party interests

40. Courts should have the power to restore prohibited goods (such as illegal drugs) to their rightful owners but only if the owner was licensed or permitted to possess them (e.g. a hospital). (p. 123).

41. In other cases property interests of third parties should be forfeited only if, before the commission of the offence, they knew or suspected that their property would be involved. (p. 124).

42. The rights of third parties should be determined by the courts. (p. 125).

43. The new power to confiscate profits of an offence should extend to their proceeds by analogy with the rights of an owner of property to 'trace' it into its proceeds. Consequently innocent third parties who have purchased the property or its proceeds should be immune for confiscation, and so, too, should *bona fide* donees who incurred expenditure or obligations in reliance on a gift. (p. 126).

44. Third parties should have a right to be heard before a restitution order is made which deprives them of their interest. Where a forfeiture order is challenged by third parties on an application under the Police (Property) Act 1897 they should be able to argue that the property was not sufficiently linked to the offence for the order to have been properly made. The alternative procedure of a county court action against the police for wrongful interference with their goods should continue to be available. Third parties should also have the

right to oppose the confiscation of their property. They ought to be able to apply for a pre-trial freezing order to be lifted in relation to their property but only if this application can be determined without prejudice to the defendant's criminal trial. (p. 127).

45. Except where possession of the property is itself an offence, the police or prosecution should advertise in an appropriate paper any forfeiture order under sect. 43 of the Powers of Criminal Courts Act 1973 where the property has a value of £1,000 or more. (p. 128).

46. Where third parties have the right to be heard they should be entitled (if otherwise qualified) to obtain legal aid. They should have a right of appeal against any order. (p. 129).

I.   Application of moneys or property received

47. Where more than one financial order has been made, the priority for the application of moneys or property received should be first the discharge of any compensation order, secondly payment of prosecution costs ordered to be paid. We propose that any other moneys such as fines or the proceeds of forfeiture or confiscation orders should be used for a Victim Compensation Fund (see 7. above). (p. 132).

J.   The relationship between monetary and proprietary orders and other penalties

48. Orders for the payment of money (e.g. by way of fine, compensation order) or the transfer of property (e.g. by way of confiscation order) should be taken into account in calculating other sentences. Such orders might properly reduce a sentence of imprisonment which would otherwise be imposed. They should however not take the place altogether of what would otherwise be a proper sentence of imprisonment unless in a borderline case the defendant has by his co-operation assisted the court in making a proprietary order. (p. 136).

49. The degree to which monetary or proprietary orders should be taken into account should depend on the sacrifice that they call for from the particular defendant, given his means. If a sentencer would regard a financial penalty as sufficient, it should be possible to tailor the total of compensation order (if any) and fine to the circumstances of the defendant, even if this meant increasing fines for wealthy defendants. Experiment with the 'day fine' system, where the penalty is calculated as a multiple of the amount which a defendant earns in a day, should be undertaken. (p. 136).

List of submissions received by the Committee in response to the consultative document

The Home Office

Professor Glanville Williams, Cambridge University

Mr Martin Wasik, University of Manchester

National Association of Probation Officers
An oral submission was also given by Mr Owen Wells of the Association

Magistrates' Association

Commissioners for the Inland Revenue, comments prepared by H.H. Monroe

Commissioners for Customs and Excise
An oral submission was also given by Mr John Sellers and Mr Downham

The Justices' Clerks' Society

The Metropolitan Police
Oral submissions were also given by Assistant Chief Constable Gerty of the West Midlands Constabulary, and Mr Michael Wilmot, a solicitor with the Metropolitan Police

National Association of Victim Support Schemes

Criminal Injuries Compensation Board
An oral submission was also given by Sir Michael Ogden QC

Association of Chief Police Officers

Insolvency Practitioners Association

The Law Society

The Law Commission

The Committee also received oral submissions from Mr Michael Crystal, a barrister specialising in insolvency, Mr Allan Green, Treasury Counsel at the Central Criminal Court and Dr Burt Galaway, an expert on US restitution schemes.

Table of Cases

General Index